MIDDLE SCHOOL
HIGH SCHOOL
COLLEGE & BEYOND

Carole Marsh's CAREERS CURRICULUM

WORK WORDS

Job / Business / Career Words & Terms You Need to Know!

CAROLE MARSH

Do yourself a favor—read this book! Nothing's more embarrassing than "getting the job" and then feeling clueless because you don't understand half of what your boss is saying!

Editor: Janice Baker
Assistant Editors: Charles Peterson
Madeline Vogler
Adrianna Atkinson
Cover Design: Lisa Kelly
Content Design: Randolyn Friedlander
Lisa Kelly
Maggie Bowers
Project Manager: Paige Muh

For additional information about Carole Marsh's Careers Curriculum or other curriculum products, contact:

Gallopade International
P.O. Box 2779
Peachtree City, Georgia 30269
800-536-2438, ext. 11
www.careerscurriculum.com
www.gallopade.com

Carole Marsh's CAREERS CURRICULUM™

Books

Essential Skills for the Real World of Work:
Things *Every* Student Must Know!

Job Tracks: 60* Great Careers—and How to Get from Where You Are...to Where You Want to Go! *Real Job Success Stories from 21st Century Career Pathways!

Would *You* Hire This Person?: A Look at Getting Hired (or Not!)... from the Point of View of Your (Possible!) Future Employer

The Parent and Teacher's Guide to Helping Students Navigate the Bumpy Road from School to More School, First Job, and Career

Business Ethics and Etiquette for Students—
You MUST Know These!

WORK WORDS: Job/Business/Career Words and Terms You Need to Know!

Also available in ebook formats

Contents

A Word from the Author

Dear Student,

You go to work.

You made good grades, you've been around, you've even had some part time babysitting or yard work, you think you're pretty smart, and you are.

But suddenly you feel insecure, unconfident, a bit "out of the loop." Why? Because you are encountering a lot of words, terms, and phrases that you've either never heard before, or just never pondered the real business world meaning of them all.

Your befuddlement might even amuse your supervisor or fellow young workers. Depending on how business vocabulary clueless you are, it might even aggravate your boss. But most of all, you're under enough stress with a new job. You don't need hesitation, embarrassment, or discomfort, especially in a meeting when these words, terms, and phrases might zip back and forth like a ball in a tennis match.

Solution: Be proactive (an Essential Skill) and learn a few of the words in this book each day. (Lifelong Learning=Essential Skill!) Trust me, there are a lot more where these came from, as well as plenty of lingo, jargon, and newfangled business and technology words coming along all the time. You might as well catch up now!

A Great Vocabulary is an Essential Skill, too!

Carole Marsh
Founder/CEO
GALLOPADE INTERNATIONAL

....and often, first-time employer!

Choose a job you love, and you will never have to WORK a day in your life.– Confucius

If you wish to know the mind of a man, listen to his WORDS.– Chinese proverb

A-Z Career Words

assets...

The collection of job-ready skills and abilities you accumulate, like good public speaking skills.

background check...

An investigation into a potential employee's past to find out if they've ever been convicted of a crime or other misdeed. Today, background checks often include checks into social media, like Facebook and Twitter, so always be careful of what you share and what your friends share about you!

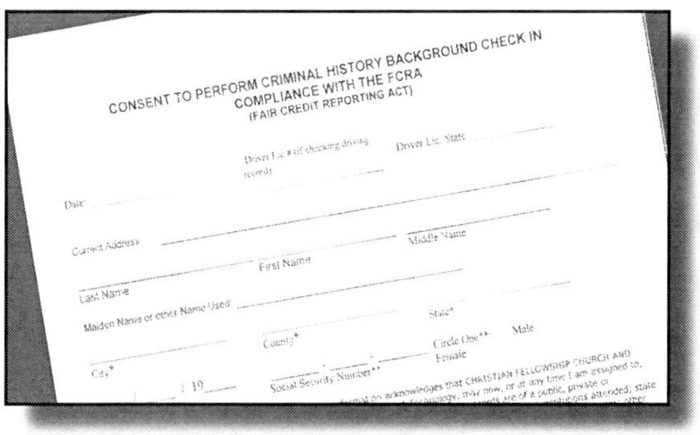

certificate...

A document that shows that you have earned the ability to do a certain job in a certain field because of specialized training or education, which may or may not include a college diploma. Teaching is an example of a career that requires college and a separate certification, while nurse's aides, pharmacy technicians, and paralegals all just need a certificate.

deduction...

An amount that may be subtracted from a total, most often used in regard to taxes.

ethics...

Principles, morals, something to live and work by—a sort of code that can help keep people out of trouble should they follow them. Examples are not cheating or stealing.

etiquette...

The proper or best way of acting, dressing, and speaking, particularly with good manners. Etiquette is extremely vital during a job interview, as first impressions are always important.

freelancer...

A self-employed person, like a writer or an artist, who is not employed continuously but hired for a specific assignment.

goal...

Something desired or wanted that is usually specific and within a certain time frame, like trying to learn Spanish by the end of the school year.

headhunter...

A person hired by a business to find a qualified individual for a specific job. Headhunters are often used to find people for high-level or hard-to-fill positions.

internship...

A role in which students or other young people inexperienced in a certain field work for a company (usually unpaid or for class credit) in order to learn about and gain experience in the area of interest.

job interview...

A method used to find out if a potential employee should be hired. Someone within the company asks questions or has a conversation with the candidate to see if they would be a good fit or not.

know-how...

The knowledge of how to do something, like computer know-how—the skill or ability to work well with computers.

letter, as in cover letter...

A letter to the person in charge of interviewing and hiring employees that briefly states why the candidate is interested and would be qualified for a certain position. Many jobs, internships, and some volunteer opportunities require such a letter because it helps the company get to know the person a bit more in depth, rather than relying only on an application or resume.

management...

The person or persons controlling or directing the affairs of a business.

networking...

The use of business connections in order to find a job, sell a product, etc.

on-the-job training...

Like it sounds, this is instruction that you receive after being hired to learn everything you'll need to know to do your job well.

portfolio...

A group of examples of your work, like photographs, artwork, or stories.

quality control...

The guidelines and rules set to make sure that everything is done in a consistent manner, like production of a product, customer service, etc. Quality control helps to ensure that your new laptop doesn't break in half after one use!

quota...

A prescribed number or quantity, as of items to be manufactured, or students admitted to a college.

references...

People you ask to give their good opinion, or a good recommendation, to someone who may want to hire you. Most applications have a section for these, which usually can't be friends or family. Better get to work impressing your teachers and others who can give you a good reference!

soft (essential) skills...

These are more who you are and how you deal with things, rather than what you know and what you can do. These would include having good time management skills more than being able to fix computers.

telecommuting...

When you work, you have some sort of commute (travel to get from home to your place of work), whether short or long. Telecommuting is the idea of working from home for a business and 'commuting' through a computer and telephone.

underemployed...

A person who has a job but is more educated than the job requires.

value-added...

An improvement that a business makes to a product in order to give it an edge over other similar and possibly identical products. An example of this is a warranty on your computer, iPod, or car. Even your messaging and data plan with your cell phone is considered a value-added service!

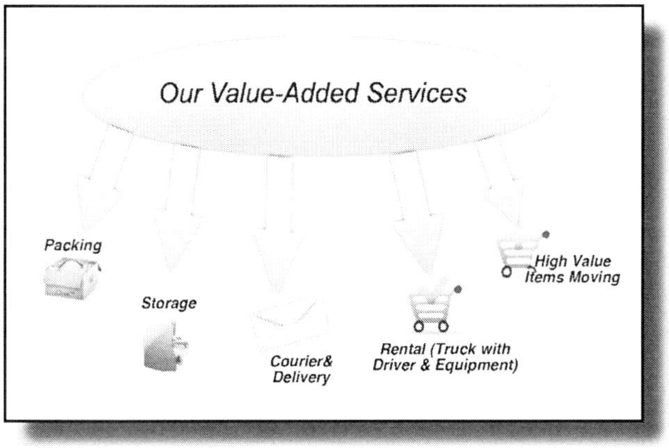

wage (or salary)...

The amount of money an employee makes for a year's worth of work.

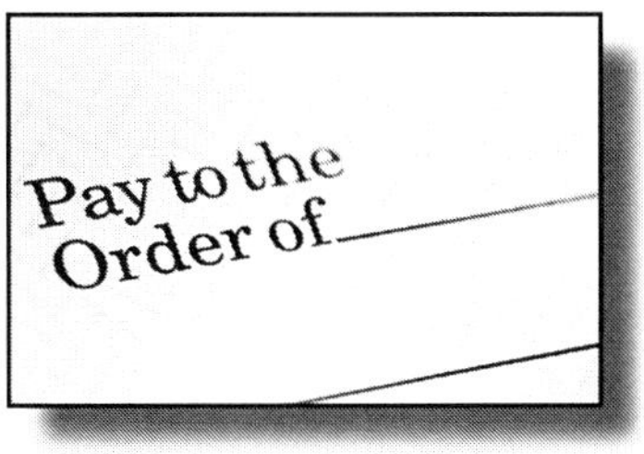

eXpectation...

The understanding that a person is likely to do something, like your employer has an expectation that you will show up to work on time.

eXecutive...

Someone exceptionally important; a higher-up within a company or business; someone in charge.

year-end...

The conclusion of a company's year-long accounting period.

zilch...

Zero error rate; the number of errors most businesses shoot for in any process or operation.

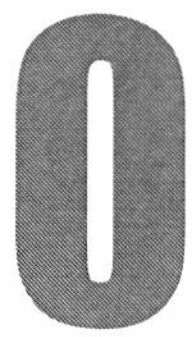

Accounting

ability to pay...

Having the necessary funds to pay, either for some sort of product, or reimburse for a debt.

account number...

The unique number given to a specific customer in order to keep it and all of its business and transaction history with the business separate from other accounts.

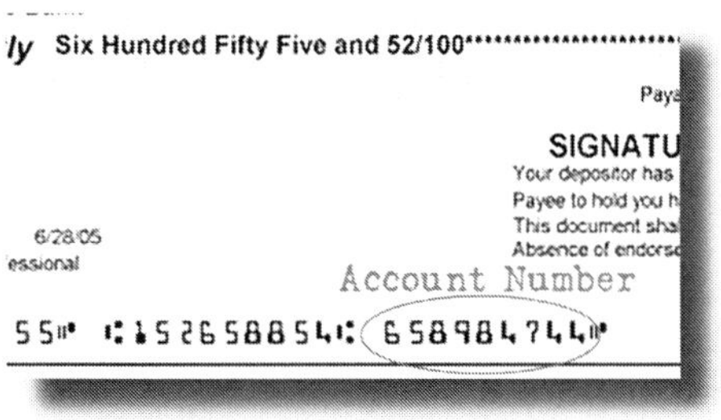

accounting cycle...

The system of keeping track of and analyzing different money transactions.

accounting error...

An unintentional mistake made in the process of analyzing and keeping track of money transactions.

accounting method...

A specific system used in order to calculate something dealing with the money transactions of a business.

accounting period...

A set amount of time used for bill and repaying.

accounting records...

The documents of the history of all monetary transactions.

accounting software...

Computer programs used in order to make accounting easier, more efficient, and more accurate. Quicken is an example.

annual earnings...

The amount of money made in a year.

annual report...

An official document that states all of the profits, losses, and other activity of a company over a year.

apportionment...

A sharing or distribution of something.

appraisal...

An assessment or review in order to find out how much something is worth. For example, jewelry and antique furniture can be appraised, among many other things.

assets...

All property that a person owns that has some sort of money value. Also, the collection of job-ready skills and abilities you accumulate, like good public speaking skills.

audit...

A review of the financial transactions of a business.

backdating...

Dating a document or transaction earlier than when it was actually executed. This can be used for financial transactions or insurance transactions, but can be illegal—so should never be done without legal approval.

bailout...

Giving a loan to a company or industry that is in financial difficulty. Most recently, the U.S. Government bailed out the banking industry and the automotive industry, calling them "too big to fail."

balance...

The final amount in an account after all subtractions and additions. If you have a personal bank account already, then you know that a positive balance is always better than a perfect or negative one!

balance sheet...

A financial document that shows every money resource of a company at the time that the document is produced.

balanced budget...

A budget that has equal amounts of income and expenses, no debt. Budgets are essential for companies and for individuals.

bankruptcy...

When a person or company runs out of money and has more debts than they can pay off, this is how they can help pay off those debts. The process needs a lawyer and legal proceedings so that the law will recognize the bankruptcy. (This requires getting a lawyer and taking legal action to make lower their responsibility or length the time frame for the due dates of these debts.)

base period...

Usually used in accounting, this is a period of time used as a reference point to compare with other periods of time. Companies use base periods to compare income and expenses from month to month or year to year.

bearer...

Someone who holds or carries something, typically something of value, bonds, for example.

bond...

A financial investment; a certificate issued when money is lent as an investment and has set terms for repayment.

bonus...

The extra money that an employee receives as some sort of perk for something, like meeting a goal.

borrower...

The person, group, or company who is loaned money and is required to pay it back. How long they have to pay it back and by how much at a time depends on each situation. So if you take out a loan to buy a house, car, or to help pay for your education, then you are the borrower!

bubble...

When the prices of assets (stock, real estate, etc) rise beyond their reasonable estimated price. Be careful! That bubble can burst, and prices will return to normal.

calendar year...

A year with 365 days, starting on January 1 and ending on December 31, according to the calendar. There are other sorts of years that businesses use, like fiscal and tax years, which generally end and begin on different dates from a regular calendar year.

capital...

The money or property a corporation owns that allows them to make transactions.

capital investment...

The money you pay for something that you really need to run your business.

cash flow...

...Into my wallet? Although that would be nice, this is actually the measure of how money moves throughout a company.

cash on hand...

The amount of physical money that a company can spend. For example, I currently have 37 cents on hand.

collateral...

Property used by a borrower as a pledge to repay a loan. Sometimes a promise just isn't enough!

compensation...

A form of payment in exchange for services or goods.

Consumer Price Index (CPI)...

This measures the changes in prices that consumers pay for a variety of products over a set amount of time, like eggs, gas, bus fare, etc.

cost of living...

How much money it takes to live, eat, entertain, and transport yourself.

credit policy...

Rules set for dealing with the lending of money to customers in order for them to purchase goods, products, or services.

deductible expenses...

The costs of a business that will not end up making more money like the costs spent on producing a product would. These can be anything from rent to electricity.

dividend...

The portion of company profits that is paid out to shareholders of company stock. Sometimes shareholders will get dividends as cash and sometimes they can automatically reinvest them to purchase more shares of stock.

dollar cost averaging...

An investment strategy where an equal amount of money is invested regularly over a set period of time, bringing down the average cost of the investment. For example, say you buy $100 worth of Coca Cola stock each month. Each month you will get differing amounts of shares because stock price fluctuates. Over the period of a year, you can determine the average price per share you paid.

EBIT (earnings before interest and taxes)...

Financial term describing a profit prior to receiving interest and paying income tax expenses.

The Economy...

The proverbial term for the state of the U.S. or world economic system. If economic indicators such as the stock market, inflation, unemployment rate, etc. are positive, we say the "The Economy" is good. If these indicators are negative, then "The Economy" is bad.

The New Economy...

The term used to describe the transition of the U.S. economic system from a manufacturing based economy to a service based economy. This transition started with the "dot-com" boom of the 1990s.

expense report...

A document that shows what has been spent on different items needed to run the business, like gas or food.

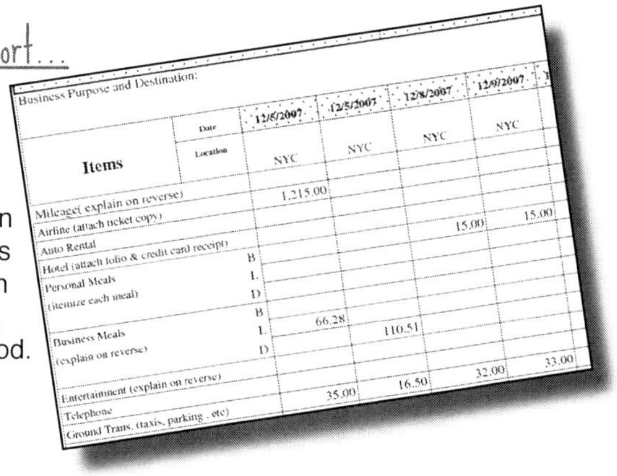

factoring...

A financial transaction where a business sells its accounts receivable to a third party at a discount.

financial projections...

A fancy word for an estimate of what a company will earn or lose.

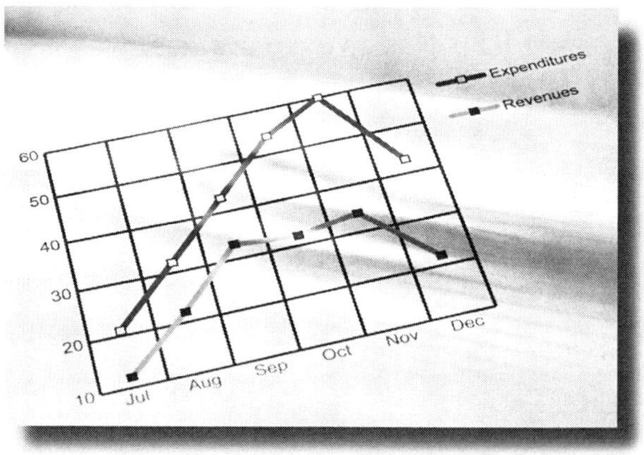

fiscal year...

The 12 month time-frame in which companies plan their budget and tax reporting. This can correlate to the calendar year (January—December), but not always. Sometimes a fiscal year can be September to August.

general ledger...

The accounting record of a business to determine its assets and liabilities. Entries are made as debits and credits, just like your checkbook register.

"in budget"...

Staying within a predetermined amount of money for a specific purpose. Like if you have a clothing budget and you've set aside $250 per year to be spent on clothes, and you don't want to spend any more than that. Easier said than done, sometimes, right?

income statement...

A usually monthly document that explains how much the company has made by listing and calculating all expenses and profits.

inflation...

When prices rise relative to the availability of goods. In other words, too much money chasing too few goods.

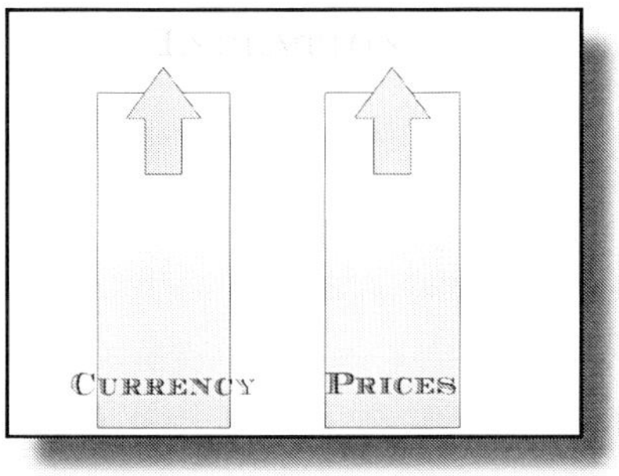

invest...

To give money to a product or company in order to make more money. This is like if your friend decides to start a new t-shirt design business and you give them money to buy the shirts in exchange for a portion of the profits later on.

invoice...

Sort of like a bill, this form shows all goods, products, or services purchased, the price of the individual products, and the total price of the order.

leverage...

A debt of some sort that a company uses for investment and improvements in order to maximize profit and efficiency.

lien...

The right to take, hold or sell the property of a debtor as payment for a debt.

line of credit...

An agreement between a company and a bank for the company to borrow money for business needs up to a pre-specified amount. Many companies can use this money to float business expenses until revenue comes in. Successful companies pay it back as quickly as possible.

margin...

The difference between the payment received for a good or service and the cost to produce or provide it.

market portfolio...

A portfolio listing every asset (every item of value) within a market sector – this can be anything from real estate to a stamp collection.

net worth...

This isn't the cost of a fishing net ... this is the amount of money that a company has that they can spend. For example, when a company pays taxes, the money they have left after paying those taxes is their net worth.

offset...

To counterbalance or compensate for something else. For example, a person may sell assets to offset expenses.

overhead...

Like 'in over my head'? Not quite. These are the costs of running a business besides those that deal with the production of a good, and can include anything from office supplies to salaries.

past due...

Payment that has not been paid by the agreed upon date.

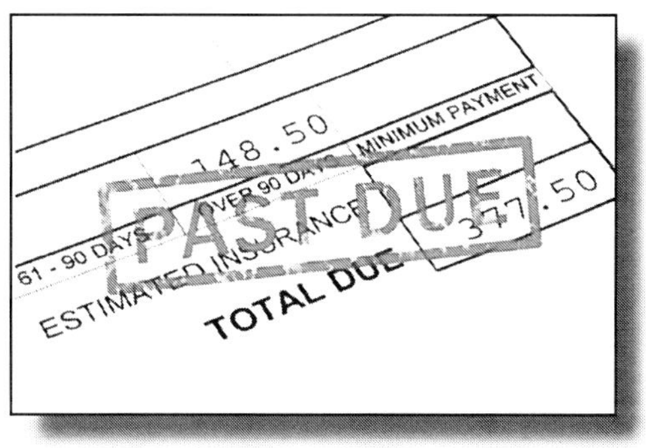

payee...

The person or company that receives a payment. If Tom writes Cindy a check for $100, Cindy is the payee.

petty cash...

Cash that a company keeps available for small transactions with customers or small business expenses, like pizza.

prequalify...

Determining the amount that a borrower can borrow before applying for a loan. Banks look at assets, liabilities, and previous borrowing history to tell if a borrower prequalifies for a loan.

prime rate...

An interest rate at which banks lend money to their best customers. If a customer's credit is excellent, they will often receive loans below prime rate.

pro forma...

Pro whata? This is a Latin phrase that means "for the sake of form." It is a type of financial statement that highlights certain numbers on the form for the company's purposes.

profit...

The amount of money that a person or company receives from the sale of a good or service after all costs of producing the good or service have been subtracted.

rebalance...

To change an amount to make the situation better overall, like rebalancing the budget to better allocate your funds.

revenue...

Money! Money! Money! The money received into a company from sales of its products or services. To be successful and profitable, businesses need more revenue than expenses. *Duh.*

running the numbers...

Also known as crunching numbers; basically, how you come up with statistics.

shoestring...

This term is used to describe a small amount of money that is considered inadequate for its intended purpose. Before you get a job, you may be living on a shoestring budget.

stakeholder...

Someone who has an investment in a business, organization, product, or industry.

valuation...

The process of determining how much an asset, company, or anything else is worth.

venture capital...

A source of financing for a start-up company that is embarking on new business or attempting to turn the business around.

windfall...

An unexpected profit or financial gain. Lottery tickets, anyone?

year-end...

Like it sounds, this is the conclusion of a year, particularly dealing with the money-related parts in a business, like accounting.

Acronyms

ASAP...

As soon as possible. This term can be used if you need information very quickly, but it doesn't have a set due date.

B2B (Business-to-Business)...

The interaction between two businesses, such as that between the manufacturer and the retailer, like when Apple and Target agree that Target can sell iPods.

B2C (Business-to-Consumer)...

The direct interaction between the purchaser of the product and the creator of the product, like when you buy an iPod directly from Apple.

BBB...

Better Business Bureau. This organization aims to promote more ethical business practices, hoping to achieve mutual trust between buyers and sellers. As a consumer, you can file a complaint that the BBB will try to resolve.

CC (Carbon Copy)...

This CC is the same CC you see next to the "To:" field in every email you write! Putting an email address here means that person will receive the email as well. In businesses, this spot is usually used for a person to whom the email is relevant but is not necessarily the intended recipient of the email.

CEO...

Also known as the Chief Executive Officer. This is an incredibly important person within the company – the head of all heads, the boss of all bosses. They can sometimes be the director on the Board of Directors, but almost always have some position on the board.

CFO...

Chief Financial Officer. The person in charge of all the financial happenings in a company.

CIO...

Chief Information Officer. This title is given to the person responsible for the information technology and computer systems within a company.

CMYK...

Cyan, Magenta, Yellow, Black. This set of colors is used to produce images for printing purposes. These pigment colors can be combined to produce any other color.

CO...

Company. Usually used as an abbreviation, but occasionally used within a company's name, such as PepsiCo or Costco.

COO...

Chief Operating Officer. The person who has responsibility for the day-to-day activities of a company.

CTO...

Chief Technology Officer. The person who oversees the technical issues within a company, including supervising the staff who build products.

D&B...

Dun & Bradstreet. A company that specializes in researching the financial reputation of companies and businesses.

EOY...

End-of-year. The end of the fiscal year, when accounts are tallied and inventories are closed.

EPS...

Earnings per share. The portion of a company's profit that is allocated to each outstanding share of stock. For example, if a company earned $10 million last year and had 10 million shares outstanding, they would report an EPS of $1 per share.

FAQ...

Frequently asked questions. These questions usually appear on a flier or website for easier access for the user to answer common questions about the product.

FDA...

Also known as the Food and Drug Administration, this is the government agency that tries to make sure all the food we eat and medicine we take are as safe as possible.

FIFO...

First in, first out. A method of keeping and evaluating inventory in which the first products placed in inventory are sold first, the second product is sold second, etc. This method is used to determine Cost of Goods Sold for a company.

FMV...

Fair Market Value. The price of a product as it passes from a willing seller to a willing buyer and when both parties know the relevant facts. If you bought your new sunglasses from Target for $9.99 but didn't know they had a scratch on them, the sunglasses were not sold at their FMV.

FTE...

Full Time Employee. Someone who works at a company 35 or more hours each week.

FYI...

For your information. A phrase used when you are providing additional information to your boss or coworker that you think they will need to know.

GAAP...

Generally Accepted Accounting Principles. Rules and procedures that describe and define accepted accounting practices, including both broad guidelines and detailed procedures.

GM...

General Manager. This person has broad responsibilities throughout the company, usually with other managers reporting to him or her.

HSA...

Health Spending Account. A savings account established by an individual specifically to hold money to be used for medical expenses. These accounts have many tax advantages.

INC...

An abbreviation for "incorporated." Many companies will be legally registered as corporations.

IPO...

Initial Public Offering. When a company offers shares of its stock for sale to the public for the very first time.

ISBN...

International Standard Book Number. A code used to track and identify books in commercial sale.

90000

9 780635 090010

LIFO...

Last in, first out. A method of inventory in which the most recent items received are considered the first items sold. Any items remaining in inventory at the end of the year are treated like they had been in the opening inventory.

LLC...

Limited Liability Company. A legal form of a company that has both partnerships and corporate structure. It is not a corporation.

LOI (Letter of Intent)...

A document outlining an agreement between two parties, but is not legally binding like a contract.

MO...

Money order. A financial object that can take the place of cash and can be exchanged for cash by the person named on the money order. These are similar to travelers' checks.

MS...

Manuscript. A written document, usually before the final draft.

MSRP...

Manufacturer's suggested retail price. The manufacturer's suggestion for what price the retailers should sell the product. It really is a suggestion; the retailer is not required to sell the product at that price.

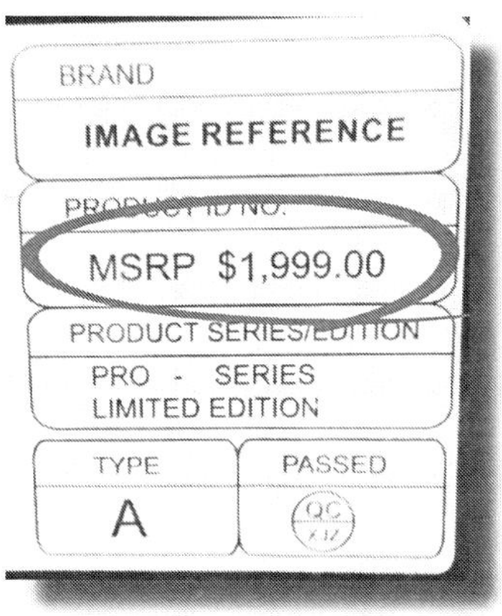

MTD/YTD...

Month-to-date/Year-to-date. A display of the accumulated accounts from the beginning of the fiscal year to the latest available period.

NDA...

Nondisclosure agreement. A contract most commonly used in companies that produce electronics in which the employees agree to not reveal information about upcoming products. These agreements help make sure that information about the new iPad updates don't get released before Apple is ready.

OTC...

Over the counter. This term describes when a buyer and seller exchange their goods over the phone or through computers rather than meeting in person.

P&L...

Profit and loss statement. This statement gives a summary of the company's gains and expenses for a designated accounting period.

PA...

Professional Association. A group of professionals within a career field who come together for professional development, networking, sharing new ideas and best practices, and representing the interests of the profession before government entities. Almost every occupation has a professional association that you can join.

PC...

This can actually stand for two things. The first is personal computer...obviously. The second is political correctness. This term describes when a person really watches their words so they don't offend anyone.

PDF/JPEG...

Electronic file types for graphics, photos, and art to be used in computer generated documents or online.

PO...

Purchase order. Authorization and agreement of a supplier to ship a product at a specified price.

POA (Power of Attorney)...

The means by which one person (the principal) can appoint another as his or her representative and grants that person the authority to perform certain acts on behalf of the principal.

POS...

Point-of-sale. This term refers to the area from which a sale is made. For example, the self-checkout at the Target and the Amazon website are both points of sale.

PTO (Paid Time Off)...

This is a program in which employees are granted or can accumulate a certain amount of hours they don't have to work but can still get paid. If you have enough PTO, you can go on vacation and still be making money!

QA/QC...

Quality Assurance/Quality Control. These two sets of activities are used to manage and assess the risks of developing and maintaining a product. QA ensures the process is efficient, and QC evaluates the actual product.

RFP (Request for Proposal)...

An invitation to a service provider or supplier to propose providing a product or service. The proposal typically outlines costs, risks, and deadlines.

RGB...

Red, Green, Blue. These are the three colors of light that can be mixed to produce any color. When designing a product for use on a TV or computer, it is important to use this color pallette.

ROI (Return on Investment)...

A ratio that measures how profitable a business is.

SBICs (Small Business Investment Companies)...

Like the name says, these are companies that give money to small businesses.

SOP...

Standard Operating Procedure. A set of given instructions you are supposed to follow in a given situation. A business may have an SOP for dealing with complaints or accepting a promotion.

STET...

This is a word used by editors to indicate that a previous mark or change should be ignored and the words should be left as is.

TBD / TBA...

To be determined; to be announced at a later time, not yet decided. If you were just assigned a project, but the due date isn't known yet, you can say the due date is TBD.

TM...

Trademark. Any logo, symbol, image, or word that identifies a company and allows the consumer to differentiate between companies. For example, a person looking for a new computer can easily tell the difference between a Microsoft laptop and an Apple laptop by the trademark images on each of the products.

UPC...

Universal Product Code. This is the number you see on the back of a product that's used to track and identify the product. The UPC can be translated into a barcode that allows for easier identification and processing.

URL...

Uniform Resource Locator. You probably use them all the time, but never knew their official name. URLs are the global address of documents and resources on the Internet, or as everyone says—a website address.

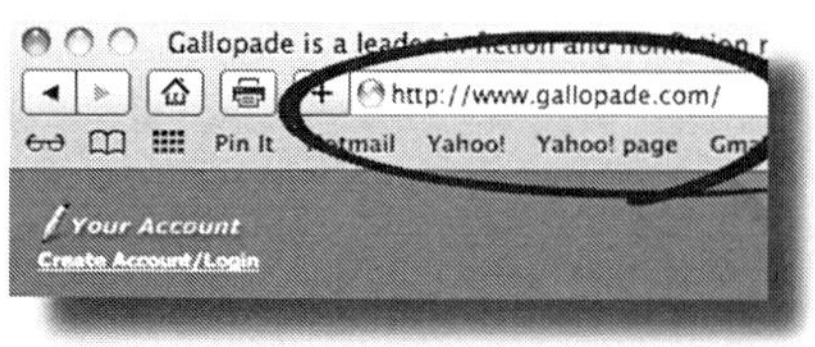

VP...

Vice President. An officer in a company ranking directly below the president, but still really important. This person will take over the president's duties if he or she is absent or ill.

WYSIWYG...

What you see is what you get.

Company Structure

The people, places, departments, and hierarchy that make up all types of businesses.

accounting...

More than just a count, this is the department in charge of the finances of the business. The Accounting Department is responsible for giving employees their paychecks.

accounts payable...

What a company owes to another group or individual, like bills.

accounts receivable...

This is any amount due to a company from any source that the company expects to be paid. An example of this is when a person gets billed a certain amount from a company, like AT&T. AT&T expects this amount to be paid to them, even before the person has paid it.

affiliated...

Associated or united in some way. Target is an example of an affiliated chain of stores.

agency...

A business group that has a specific purpose, usually hired by a company to represent and coordinate all of its business dealings in a certain area—like an insurance agency or advertising agency.

ancillary...

Someone who provides necessary support for the activities and operations of a business or industry.

association...

The relationship of a group of people with a common purpose.

back office...

The departments and tasks in a company that are dedicated to making that company run—accounting, administration, and product development are examples. Though these departments are not prominently seen by customers, they are essential to the company's success.

blue collar...

Although this is used in order to help identify your beloved dog or cat, in the business world, this is someone who does physical work as part of his or her job, like in construction.

board of directors...

A board of dictators? Not really. This is a group of people who have been selected to make decisions and determine policies, rules, and guidelines to make sure that a company runs as smoothly as it can.

brick-and-mortar...

The physical location of a business that meets with its customers face to face. A grocery store, a hair salon, and a restaurant are all examples of this kind of business.

business day...

The period of time when a company and its employees conduct their business and do their work.

centralize...

When the activities of an organization or department become concentrated to one certain location or under one entity (like the government).

chairman...

The head of the Board of Directors, this person holds the most power and responsibility of all the Board.

champion...

A person who strongly supports an idea, product, or policy and works to force it to implementation.

corporate culture...

The customs and beliefs of companies that have come about as time has passed and company practice has changed and evolved.

corporation...

A company that is seen legally as one 'person,' even though a group of people (the Board of Directors) are in charge of it, like Wal-Mart, Bank of America, and Microsoft, among many, many others.

customer...

The person who really signs your paycheck! The client or buyer of a company's goods or services. Without them, there will be no revenue to fund your paycheck!

customer relations...

The process of handling relationships with customers in a manner that will have them continue their business with the company. If a business has an unsatisfied customer, for example, the company will try to make the customer as happy as they can in order to keep their business.

customer service...

The department that deals with customer feedback (positive or negative) about something dealing with the business. When you have to return something you purchased at a store, you generally deal with Customer Service.

decentralize...

When the activities of an organization or department disperse from one certain location or entity (like the government) to individual entities.

director...

Similar to the ones in Hollywood, this is a person who is in charge. However, for the purposes of this book, she or he is a member of the Board of Directors.

empower/empowerment...

A form of management when employees are granted some management abilities, like making decisions.

entrepreneur...

A person who begins a business and assumes responsibility for it, including any risks that the person may face because of the business. Your friend Rodrigo, with the t-shirt business, is the entrepreneur, because he may not sell a single shirt even after he's spent 20 hours and $400 making them.

executive...

Someone exceptionally important; a higher up within a company or business; someone in charge.

franchising...

When a company has made itself available to be owned by other people in different locations but under the company's name, logo, and products. The company helps the owners run the business in various ways in exchange for a certain percentage of the profits. The businesses can be anything from restaurants, like Subway and Dunkin Donuts, to hotels, like Holiday Inn.

front office...

The departments in a company that tend to deal with customers or clients.

home office...

A place designated at home for an employee to do work, rather than go into an office, or the main office of a company.

human resources...

The department that directly deals with the employees. They take care of hiring, training, and evaluating people, insurance, salary, and anything else that has to do with the well-being and benefits of the employees. If you've ever applied for a job, particularly within a larger company or corporation, then someone in this department probably interviewed you! If you haven't yet, you probably will someday down the road.

incorporation...

The legal process of making a company a corporation.

information technology (IT)...

The department that deals with computers, telephones, Internet, media, and any other resources that use technology and helps solve any problems that may occur during normal business activities.

infrastructure...

The physical and organizational services and facilities that are needed in order for a company to function.

joint venture...

Some sort of project taken on by more than one business, person or organization, like when the Harry Potter series and the Universal Studios theme park teamed up to create the Wizarding World of Harry Potter.

management...

The people responsible for making sure that everything runs smoothly, especially when the owner or Big Boss can't or wouldn't want to. If you've ever had a part time job, then you almost certainly had a manager who oversaw your duties and job performance.

marketing...

The department in charge of advertising, packaging, delivering, and communicating in order to help a product or service sell. You can thank them for all of the commercials you see when watching TV!

merger...

When two or more companies come together under one company in order to better produce their products or services, like when Facebook bought Instagram in 2012.

mission statement...

A phrase that states the company's purpose in business, like their goals, for example.

mogul...

A really important and powerful person who is successful in his/her business and industry. Facebook's Mark Zuckerberg or billionaire Warren Buffett are good examples.

non-profit corporation...

A company that's main purpose is to somehow be beneficial to the public rather than make a profit. In exchange, it receives certain benefits from the government, like not having to pay taxes. The American Red Cross, Habitat for Humanity, Amnesty International, and World Wildlife Fund are all examples.

office politics...

This refers to how employees interact within a company and how they gain power over one another.

organization chart (org chart)...

A diagram that shows who reports to whom, showing the relationship of leaders and bosses in the company. If you're the Vice President of the company, you would be very close to the top of the chart, with all of your superiors above you and everyone else listed below you.

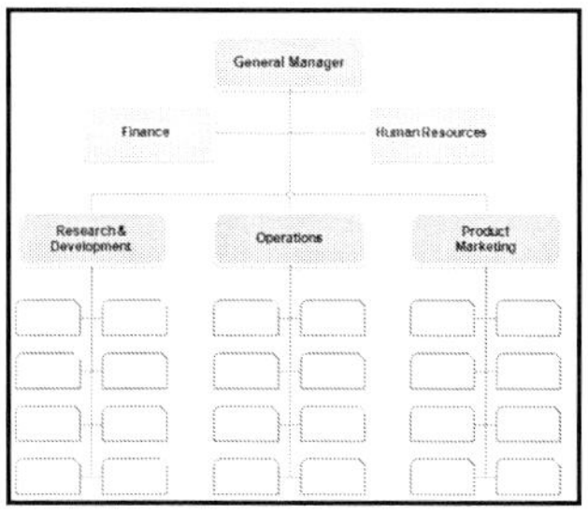

private company...

The opposite of a public company, this is a company that only has private investors and is not open to the public. Examples include Mars (the company responsible for M&M's, Snickers, etc.) and LEGO (as in the toy).

production...

The department that sees to the actual creation of a product.

public company...

Like it sounds, this is a company that the general public can invest in. Some public companies include Wal-Mart and Apple.

purchasing...

The department that buys everything that a company needs to run smoothly, like office supplies or electricity.

research and development (R&D)...

The department that oversees the development of new products and improvements on current ones through various methods of research, based on what is thought to be most appealing to consumers.

sales...

This is the department that focuses on finding someone to buy the product. Think of those pesky telemarketers or persistent car salesmen.

service provider...

Any company that provides a certain type of service, like T-Mobile provides cell phone service.

service worker...

These are the people who provide labor services, like housekeepers and lawn maintenance workers.

shareholder...

Any person or group that has financially invested in the company and will face either profit or loss depending on how the company performs. Going back to Rodrigo's t-shirt business, since you gave him some money for the business, you are a shareholder!

sole proprietorship...

The opposite of a corporation, this is when a company belongs to its owner and does not have its own legal rights. Your local, family-owned pizzeria is an example.

start up...

The very first stage of a new business venture, when it is just starting to exist.

team, team-based, teamwork...

You may be on one team, or many teams, or many teams at a time; the team is a unit with a task, budget, and deadline You need to learn to be a good teammate and team leader.

virtual office...

Conducting business and live communications offsite from a business location, alleviating traditional office expenses. Working from home is a typical virtual office.

white collar...

The type of work that does not require physical work, like administration.

Human Resources

401(k)...

A type of retirement plan that takes a portion of the salary before taxes and saves it for use only after retirement.

401(k) match...

When the company you work for is willing to contribute to your 401(k) plan, too. It's like getting free money!

age discrimination...

Prejudice against a person due to their age. The law protects anyone over 40 from age discrimination.

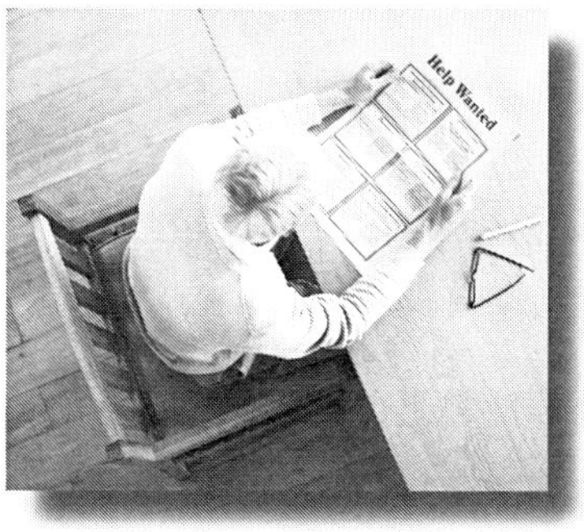

annual wage...

The amount of money an employee makes for a year's worth of work. This is also known as a salary.

back pay...

The compensation owed to an employee from some previous work or from an increase in pay.

background check...

An investigation in a potential employee's past in order to find out if they've ever been convicted of a crime or anything like that. Nowadays, these can also and usually do include checks into social media, like Facebook and Twitter, so always be careful of what you share and what your friends share about you!

base pay rate...

An employee's initial rate of compensation before bonuses, commissions, or raises.

benefits...

As far as employment goes, job benefits generally include vacations, holidays, and insurance, among others.

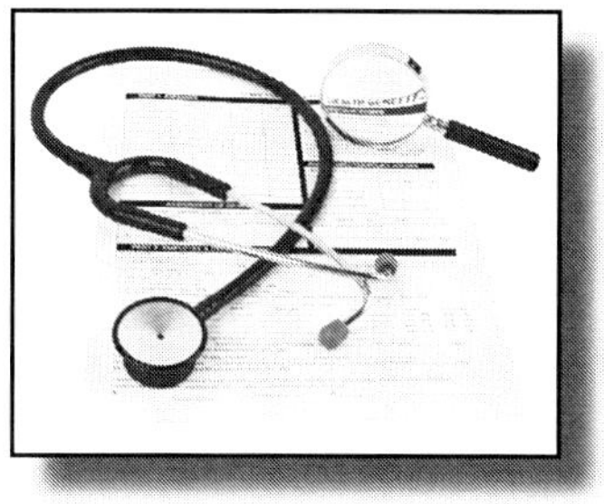

cross training...

(But not the shoes!) When an employee is trained in more than one field in order to make them a more efficient worker, like if you are technically a salesperson, but you are also trained to hire new employees.

curriculum vitae (CV)...

A longer version of a resume, with more details on educational, academic, and professional experiences. These are typically only used for jobs in the academic and science professions, which required more details.

deduction...

Can be for taxes, but also relates to any expenses, such as deductions for insurance.

disability insurance...

Insurance that covers an employee's income against the risk of a disability that makes working and earning a living impossible.

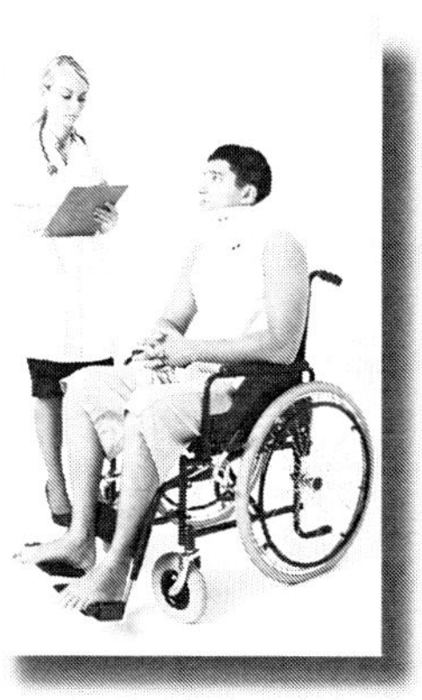

discrimination policy...

A set of rules that protect employees and future employees from being treated differently in the workplace due to race, religion, gender, sexual orientation, age, disability, or anything else.

diversity...

The state of being varied and different. For example, many colleges and workplaces today are in search of a diverse group of people for their schools or companies.

downsizing...

The process of limiting something, usually employees, in order to help lower costs. This has been especially common recently due to economic troubles.

employee manual...

A guide to the official rules and policies that employees need to know upon working at a place. These rules can include dress code and activities that are not allowed at work, among other things.

employment contract...

A legal document that contains the conditions of an employee's job, including specific duties and salary or wages.

exempt employee...

An employee who is exempt from minimum wage and overtime laws.

exemption...

In HR, this is an employee who is 'exempt' (or excused) from overtime policies because of their type of job, meaning their work doesn't have to be completed in a certain amount of time, like with management positions.

exit interview...

A meeting between an employee who is leaving the company for some reason and a manager, human resource personnel, or other company official who finds out the reason for the employee's leaving and discusses their time with the company and in their job.

Fair Labor Standards Act...

The legal act that helps make sure that employees have safe and fair working conditions and experiences. These laws include the minimum wage and child labor laws.

flex-time...

A variable work schedule an employee is allowed to work. If a company has a standard workday from 9 a.m. to 5 p.m., an employee may be allowed to work from 7 a.m. to 3 p.m. as long as his/her job is getting done.

freelancer/independent contractor...

A person hired for a specific job but not technically hired by the company; writers and graphic artists are two examples.

group health insurance...

An insurance plan that provides insurance to a select group of people—typically provided by a company to its employees.

HR managers...

People who are in charge of managing the Human Resources department and all that it deals with.

insourcing...

Using a person inside the company for some sort of project, rather than hiring someone outside of the company.

internship...

A role within a company for students or other young people inexperienced in a certain field where they work for the company, usually unpaid or for class credit, in order to learn about and get some experience in their area of interest.

job-costing...

The process of tracking the expenses incurred on a job against the revenue produced by that job.

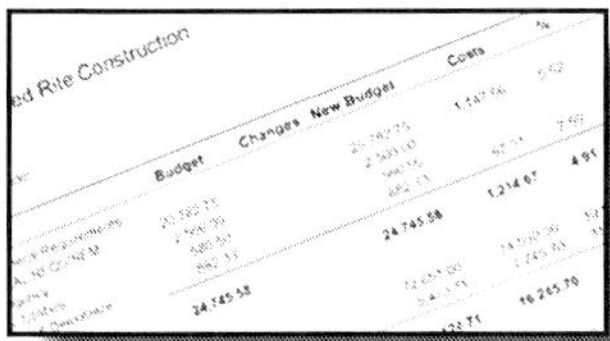

job-sharing...

When two people share a job made for one person.

labor laws...

A set of policies in rules set in place in order to make the workplace safer and fairer for all employees. Examples of these laws include a set minimum wage, anti-discrimination policies, and anti-harassment policies.

labor union...

An organized group of employees that makes sure that they are receiving proper wages and working in reasonable and safe conditions. Sometimes, this causes employees to go on strike when they are unhappy with something. When the television writers called a strike a few years back, we did not have new episodes of all of our favorite shows for a while.

man-hour...

The amount of work produced by a person in one hour.

minimum wage...

The lowest amount of money that an employee can legally be paid by their employer. There are some exceptions, like waiters and waitresses, who also receive tips in addition to their pay. Today's minimum wage is $7.25 per hour, which is loads more than the quarter an hour wage when the law was first created!

non-exempt employee...

Employees subject to the wage and hour laws established by the Fair Labor Standards Act.

notice...

As in 'two weeks'? Yes! This is the warning an employee gives to the employer warning of the employee's desire and intent to quit or resign.

on-the-job training...

Like it sounds, this is instruction that you receive after being hired to learn everything you'll need to know to do the job well.

open enrollment...

A period of time when employees of a company can enroll in the group insurance plan or other benefit plans offered to them.

outsourcing...

In order to take advantage of cheaper labor and/or production costs, the movement of some part of a company to a different location, especially a different country, or the use of person outside of the company for a specific job.

overtime...

The amount of time an employee works beyond normal working hours. Depending on the type of employee, additional wages can be paid for this time.

overtime regulations...

Rules and laws in order to protect the employees' best interests when it comes to working more hours than the normal full-time week (40 hours per week).

pension...

An arrangement to provide regular income to an employee after he/she is no longer working, such as after retirement.

performance review...

An evaluation of how efficiently something or someone works. A performance review can be done to make sure a product works as well as it should; it's the same for an employee!

Peter Principle...

The idea that employees may eventually be promoted to a level past their skills and abilities.

recruit...

The process of finding new employees. This term is usually associated with groups like the Army or Navy, but other hiring companies can also use it.

resign...

To quit or leave a job or position.

retainer fee...

A work-for-hire agreement between two parties where one party pays in advance for work to be done at a later date; usually if you hire an attorney, you must pay in advance to retain his/her services.

retirement...

The point in which an employee stops work completely, either because they have reached a certain age or have worked a certain period of years.

retirement plans...

Many ways of saving money for the future after someone has retired from their job and can no longer rely on the paycheck from that job.

severance pay...

After someone has lost their job, this is the money they receive for a certain amount of time afterward until they can find another job.

stock option...

Shares of stock granted by a company to an employee to encourage the employee to work to boost the company's value and stock price. The employee is able to purchase the shares at a fixed price, with incentive to sell for profit if the market price of the stock is higher than the fixed purchase price. Stock options are often part of executive compensation packages.

tax...

Pay "the Man!" Financial obligations to be paid to the government based on income and revenue. Companies and citizens spend a lot of time and money to determine how much they have to pay in taxes each year.

tax forms...

The multiple forms used to record and pay taxes. There are also forms to fill out to determine what taxes you will pay as an employee or business owner and how your income will be reported to the government. Here are some examples:
W-2: A federal tax form issued by employers stating how much an employee was paid in wages, salaries, and tips within a year.
W-4: A tax form used to determine the amount of taxes to be withheld from an employee's wages each pay period.
W-9: A tax form requesting a taxpayer's identification number. Typically filled out when an employee is hired for a job.
1099: A tax form that records a taxpayer's income that is other than wages, salaries, and tips.

telecommuting...

When you work, you have some sort of commute (travel to get from home to your place of work), whether short or long. Telecommuting is the idea of working from home for a business and 'commuting' through a computer and telephone.

unemployment compensation...

A set fee paid to former employees if their job is terminated. The fee is paid for a certain amount of time after their last day on the job.

vesting...

To receive an immediate and secured right to an asset; it cannot be taken away. If offered, employees can vest into stock options or pension plans after working at a company for a certain number of years.

wellness programs...

Programs designed in order to help employees learn about staying healthy, like when a school has an anti-drug week or a company has a display or fair dedicated to healthy living.

Insurance

act of God...

Any sort of natural disaster or random event that causes something negative to happen. This is usually a term in some contracts that helps one party out if something uncontrollable happens and they are not fit to finish their part of the deal. An example could be a fire or earthquake.

actuary...

Someone who uses math and statistics to determine risk, primarily in the insurance industry. For example, someone who determines how likely you are to get sick if they provide you health insurance.

assumption of risk...

Knowing that something could happen and taking responsibility for it beforehand. For example, if you know that you could get hurt while bungee jumping, but you sign the waiver saying you will not sue the company in case it does, you have assumed the risk.

beneficiary...

Some person or entity that receives money or benefits from another person or entity. The beneficiary of a life insurance policy is the person who will receive money at the death of the insured party.

business liability insurance...

Insurance provided to protect the business from lawsuits or legal claims.

claim...

This is when a person or group asks the insurance company for payment of something that is included under the insurance plan, like when you go to the doctor for something and your parents ask the insurance company to pay part or all of the bill.

liability...

Being responsible if something bad happens, like if a store leaves a puddle of slippery liquid in the middle of the floor and you slip in it and hurt yourself, they would be responsible. Or if your Xbox were to somehow cause an earthquake or a fire due to faulty manufacturing, then the makers of Xbox would be in trouble (this is technically an example of product liability).

premium...

An amount paid in installments for a insurance policy.

risk management...

The process of trying to find any possible problems and solutions to the problems before they occur, so that any problems can be handled quickly and efficiently. This could mean planning firewalls or fire escape routes ahead of time or having a backup phone or Internet line.

umbrella policy...

Insurance that covers amounts above what is normally covered in a company's primary insurance policies.

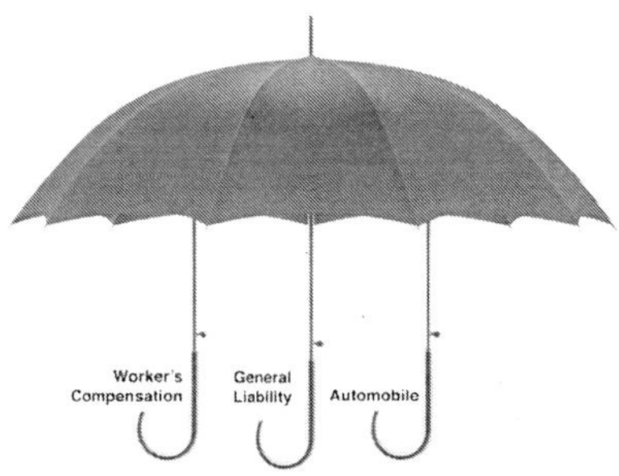

Interview • Job Search

amenities...

Features that increase attractiveness or value. For example, you may prefer a job at a company that offers its employees amenities such as free meals and a workout gym.

apprenticeship...

Working for a specific period of time for a skilled craftsman or trade worker in order to learn how to perform the job and perform it well. Apprenticeships typically happen in vocational careers.

background check...

Used often in screening job candidates, this is an investigation into a person's (or business entity's) criminal, financial, and public records. For the best chance at a great job, keep your nose clean!

certificate...

Document that shows that you have earned the ability to do a certain job in a field because of specialized training or education, which may or may not include a college diploma. One job that does require college and a separate certification is teacher. Nurse's aides, pharmacy technicians, and paralegals all just need a certificate.

commute...

The distance you travel between your home and your place of work.

cover letter...

A letter to the person in charge of interviewing and hiring employees that briefly states why the candidate is interested and would be qualified for a certain position. Many jobs, internships, and some volunteer opportunities require such a letter because it helps the company get to know the person a bit more in depth, rather than relying only on an application or resume.

due diligence...

Investigation and research on a topic. Before an interview with a potential employer or before you attempt to go into business, you should do research to show your knowledge and interest in that company or business.

expectation...

Anything wanted or desired. Your employer will expect you show up to work on a regular basis.

finder's fee...

Money paid to someone for recommending a job candidate who is ultimately hired.

five-year plan...

Where do you see yourself in five years? This is a common interview question and one for which you better have an answer! Your answer tells employers about your plans, your ambitions, and your interest in future work.

goal...

Something desired or wanted that is usually specific and within a certain time frame, like wanting to be a art director in 5 years.

headhunter...

A person hired by a business to find a qualified individual for a specific job. Headhunters are often used to find people for high-level or hard-to-fill positions.

internship...

Working for a specific period of time for a business or company to gain experience in a specific field. Work is typically done for free or cheap in exchange for valuable experience. Often, businesses will hire interns for paid jobs if the intern proves to be a good worker.

job description...

A list of tasks, functions, and requirements for a particular job.

job interview...

A method used to find out if a potential employee should be hired. Someone within the company asks questions or has a conversation with the candidate to see if they would be a good fit or not.

job posting...

The method a company or employer uses to tell current employees or the public about job vacancies. The posting should list the job description.

job shadowing...

A program where someone, usually a student, will follow a worker in a specific job for a period of time. Job shadowing makes it possible for the student to determine whether he/she is interested in that job.

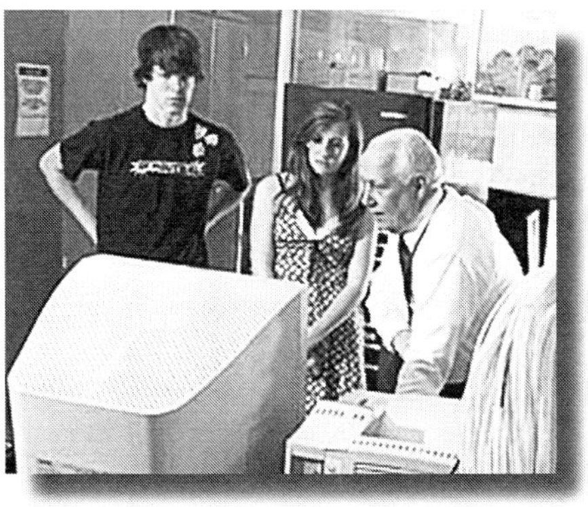

job title...

The name of a specific job or position within a business. Job titles are relative to the type of business—like Chief Executive Officer of a Fortune 500 Company or Chief Pooper Scooper of a dog walking business!

lateral move...

Changing from one job to another that is similar in level, salary, and responsibility.

learning curve...

The time that it takes for you to get proficient at the job you are doing. Employers understand that it will take time for you to learn the ropes when you start a job, and always want workers who will learn them quickly!

mentor...

Someone who is a trusted counselor or teacher in a work setting. Someone who will advise you and guide you in your occupation.

network (networking)...

The use of business connections in order to find a job, sell a product, etc., like if you used your friend's birthday party in order to find someone to hire you.

offer letter...

A formal letter from an employer to a job candidate offering a job and outlining the requirements for the job, such as its salary, and other terms of employment. Usually you have to sign the letter to show you accept the job offer.

orientation...

The period of time when a new employee is introduced to co-workers, learns company policies and procedures, and tours the facility.

portfolio...

A group of examples of your work, such as photographs, artwork, or stories.

promotion...

Taking a job or position that is higher in salary, title, and responsibility than the one you currently hold.

recruiter...

See "headhunter." The only difference between a recruiter and a headhunter is in how they get paid by the businesses they work for. Recruiters tend to be on paid contract with companies to continuously look for qualified workers. Headhunters tend to be paid only when they place a qualified worker at a company.

references...

People you ask to give their good opinion, or a good recommendation, to someone who may want to hire you. Most applications have a section for these, which usually can't be friends or family. Better get to work on impressing your teachers and others like that!

referral...

To give a recommendation about a job or a qualified candidate for a job. You have a competitive edge if someone refers you for a job. Also, some companies will pay current employees a small fee for referring qualified workers for a job opening.

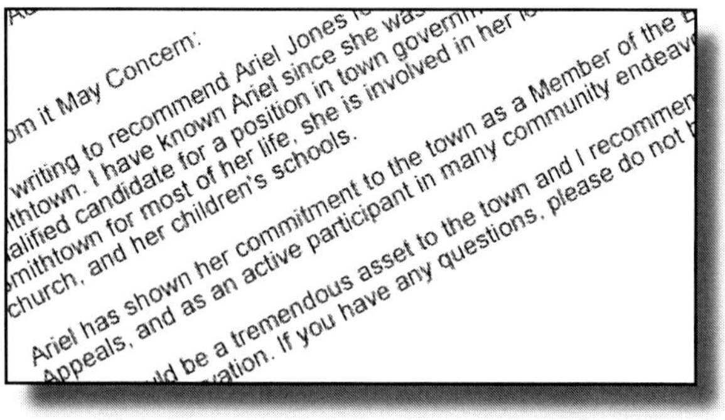
om it May Concern:
writing to recommend Ariel Jones
ithtown. I have known Ariel since she was
alified candidate for a position in town governm
mithtown for most of her life, she is involved in her
church, and her children's schools.
Ariel has shown her commitment to the town as a Member of the
Appeals, and as an active participant in many community endeav
ld be a tremendous asset to the town and I recommen
vation. If you have any questions, please do not

salary...

The fixed compensation paid to an employee on a regular basis.

temp to perm...

Starting a job in a temporary position for a short period of time, such as 90 days. During this time, your work performance will be evaluated. At the end of the temporary period, the employer will either hire you for a permanent position or end the job.

underemployed...

A person who has a job but is more educated or trained than the job requires.

OPEN FOR BUSINESS...

We did our **business plan**...**bootstrapped** our **start-up money**...got our **business license**. It was a big help to use the **SBA (Small Business Administration)** for lots of info and ideas; they were very helpful. We decided to join the chamber **(Chamber of Commerce)** so we could learn more and **network** with other **entrepreneurs**.

Soon we had our **ribbon cutting** and were open for business! Next came a flurry of opening a **commercial account** at our new bank...interviewing **job candidates** to fill our **organization chart**...writing an **employee manual**...setting up **payroll**, **accounts payable**, and **accounts receivable**, and other accounting systems. We did a **budget** with **revenue** and **expense projections** and a company calendar of **staff meetings**, **quarterly meetings**, month-end **financial reports**, and more.

We did **flow charts** for our various processes, checked our legal **compliance** with all things legal, and most of all hoped we would make a **profit** and not be **"in the red"** for too long. Planning for success, we hoped to find **venture capital** or an **"angel"** to help us through the next stage of growth.

In the meantime, isn't it time for lunch yet?!

Legal

addendum...

An addition to a legal contract.

affidavit...

A legal and official statement that has been sworn to. Like an oath, this is a statement that someone has sworn to in front of an official, like a notary public, and is legally binding.

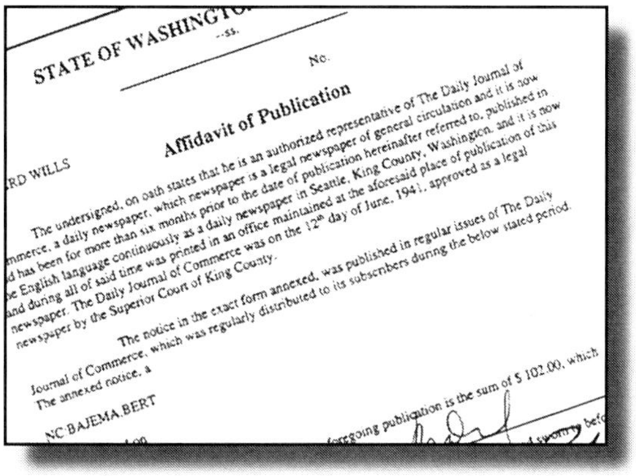

affreightment...

A contract between a ship owner and a goods owner to carry that cargo on his ship to a destination.

agreement...

Like an old-time marriage, both "parties" have to say "I do," or at least sign the contract. An Agreement happens when two groups (two people, companies, countries) agree on some business arrangement. Can we agree to disagree? Of course! But that's not always a happy marriage. Any action against the arrangement is kinda like cheating...someone's going to get hurt—usually in the pocketbook.

air rights...

The privilege of the ownership of the air above a certain property.

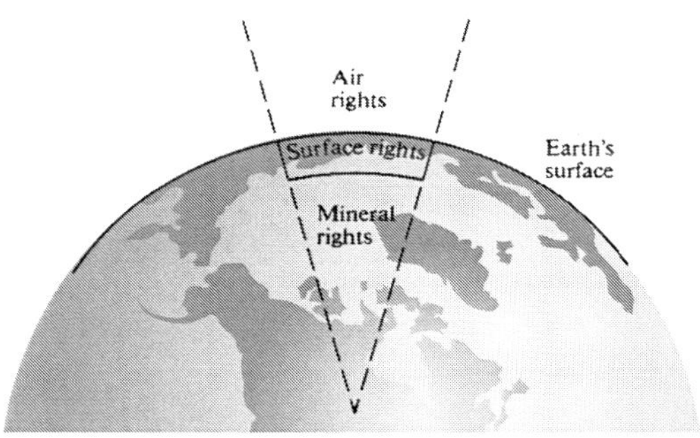

alias...

Another name that a person or company goes by. Some famous musical examples include Katy Perry for Katheryn Hudson, Diddy for Sean Combs, etc.

amend...

To change or improve something. Think of the Amendments to the *U.S. Constitution*.

annexation...

The incorporation of one piece of land into another piece of land, usually for business or political reasons. A city might want to annex nearby neighborhoods into their city limits in order to have a larger population or obtain tax dollars.

appendix...

This isn't an organ you can live without. An appendix is additional material added to the end of a contract or book. Sometimes called an "addendum" – pretty simple, huh? Add(to the)endum of a contract. Don't skim over it, there's vital information there!

arbitration/mediation...

This is how many conflicts within and between companies get resolved. People from the two sides of an argument pick a third, impartial party to decide the answer for them.

article...

News article? No. A statement or stipulation in a business contract. If your job is a game and the contract is the gameplan, then articles are the specific "rules" of the game. What, when, where and how can you play the game? Follow the rules, do it well, and you might just be the next Mia Hamm or Kevin Durant, or a business equivalent.

breach (of contract or warranty)...

When a part of a contract or warranty is violated or not honored by one of the parties in the contract or warranty.

business licenses...

The legal documents that give a company or person the right to own and operate a business in a certain location, similar to how a driver's license gives a person the right to drive.

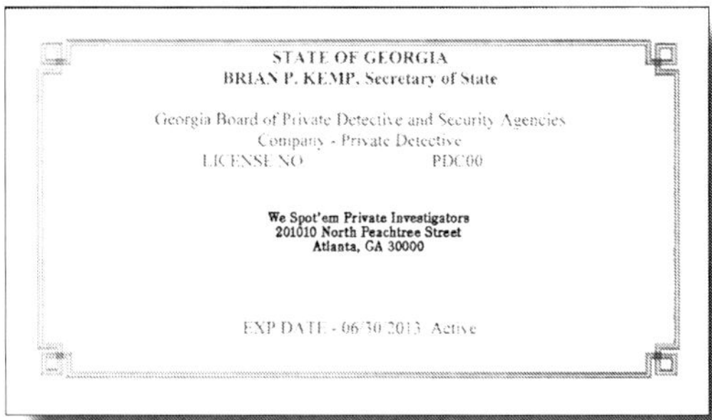
STATE OF GEORGIA
BRIAN P. KEMP, Secretary of State

Georgia Board of Private Detective and Security Agencies
Company - Private Detective
LICENSE NO PDC00

We Spot'em Private Investigators
201010 North Peachtree Street
Atlanta, GA 30000

EXP DATE - 06/30/2013 Active

business permits...

The legal documents that give a company or person the evidence of safety in their products, goods, or services and their building. You can see this in action when you see the grade a restaurant has gotten after its inspection.

by-laws...

A set of rules that govern an organization.

clause...

(not Santa) A section of a legal document.

contract...

This is the deal (period). Sign your life away. If your job is like a game, then the contract is the game-plan. How long will you work for that employer? How much money will you make? What are your responsibilities? To "contract" means "binding"—all the restricting ropes and red tape saying what you can and cannot do. Break those restrictions, and you're FREE! But you probably won't have a job, and you may get sued.

copyright...

Although to some this may read, "Copy, right?" this is actually the legal right to a product or idea, like in movies, music, or books that limits use by others and requires some sort of payment for others to use them.

©

force majeure...

An unexpected or uncontrolled event. This is something no legal contract can account for.

government contract...

The arrangement between the government and a business that details their business relationship. This could be when the government has to supply or buy a certain product or material to or from the company.

government grant...

A set amount of money given to a group by the government in order to help pay for the expenses of research or another project. For example, a southeastern U.S. company was given a grant to run a game that gave citizens money that could only be used at certain local stores in order to help the local businesses.

grandfather clause...

A provision in a contract or law that exempts those who are already involved in a certain business or activity from the provisions in that contract or law.

grant proposal...

A request or application for money from the government or some other supporter for a project, usually used by nonprofits.

hold harmless...

To release from accountability or responsibility for something.

intellectual property ...

The concept that a person's ideas and thoughts belong to that person and cannot be taken by someone else. For example, if you have the idea for a fabulous new app, by this concept, it belongs to you and you alone.

just cause...

The burden of proof an employer may need to show prior to terminating an employee. This proof protects workers from being let go for arbitrary reasons.

lease...

A contract where one person or entity allows another person or entity to use an asset (usually property) for a certain period of time and for a certain amount of money.

loophole...

A way of escaping the regulations of a contract because of poor wording within the contract itself.

null and void...

Sounds like some Emo people I know... "my life is soooo empty and sad, null and void." But in business, null and void means that a contract is invalid, not binding, without legal force. Breaking a contract's rules might mean an employer can refuse to pay you! So, like some people feel their lives amount to nothing, a contract that is null and void really is nothing, just a piece of flat wood-fiber and ink.

paralegal...

A person trained to handle legal work, but not educated or licensed as a lawyer.

party...

Person (or persons) forming one side of some argument. A party can be one person, a company, or a group with something in common, (ex: shareholders). Think Democrats and Republicans are opposing political "parties." I know, parties with strobe lights and rave music are more fun, but it's almost the same thing. These party people want something (often money), and those party people just want to dance. Remember, strength in numbers, the more the merrier.

patents...

A legal way of protecting an idea that someone has from someone else trying to use and sell it for his or her own gain. These can be given for almost any idea, including a foldable bicycle or even a blanket with sleeves.

permit...

An official record that shows that a person or company is allowed to do something. For example, in many states, teenagers need a learner's permit to allow them the right to learn how to drive.

pro bono...

Legal work done, not for compensation, but for public good.

redact...

To prepare a document for publication by editing or amending part of the document. Confidential documents are often redacted prior to being released to the public.

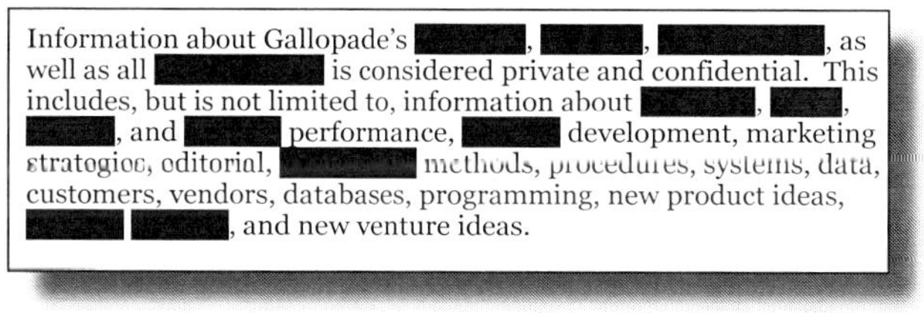

Information about Gallopade's █████, █████, █████, as well as all █████ is considered private and confidential. This includes, but is not limited to, information about █████, █████, █████, and █████ performance, █████ development, marketing strategies, editorial, █████ methods, procedures, systems, data, customers, vendors, databases, programming, new product ideas, █████ █████, and new venture ideas.

regulations...

Many business practices have all kinds of state, federal, food (FDA), etc. "regulations" lurking in the background. They're rules, laws, or policies used to keep things safe and fair.

rescind...

To annul or make void.

terms...

Like Articles, terms are rules, conditions, or stipulations in a contract. Contracts are relationships so avoid bad blood, or spilling any. Understanding the terms will help you stay on good terms with your employer.

trademark...

Any logo, word, design, image, or symbol used by a company in order to differentiate its products from others that are also being sold. McDonald's Golden Arches are an excellent example of this, as many people are exposed to them at a young age and can distinguish it from Burger King even before they learn to read!

waiver...

To defer or relinquish a claim or right to something.

zoning...

Designating land use for specific purposes. The government regulates zoning so that compatible uses of land stay in the same area—and so you don't have a landfill built next to your house!

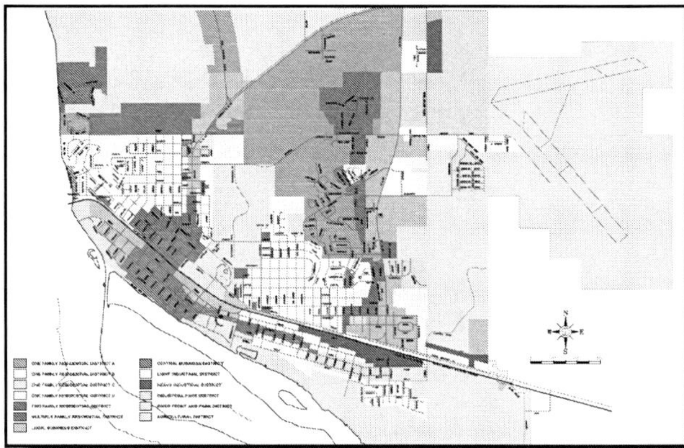

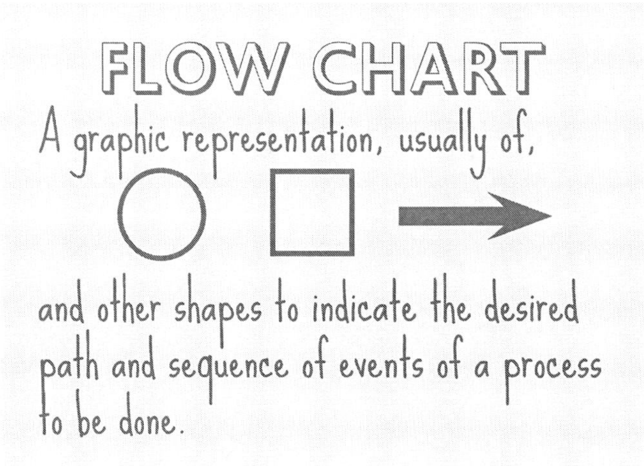

Manufacturing • Production • New Product Development

absolute advantage...

When someone, like a company or country, is able to make a product or good for less money than any other company or country. For example, if the Cool Computer Company can produce computers for a lot less than Totally Technological, Inc, then Cool Computer Company is said to have an absolute advantage over computers.

algorithm...

Although it sounds like Al-Gore-Ithim, this has nothing to do with our former Vice President. Instead, this is a pattern, or a model, that shows how something should be completed by steps. Many computer programmers use these to program computers. Solving a Rubik's cube requires one, too.

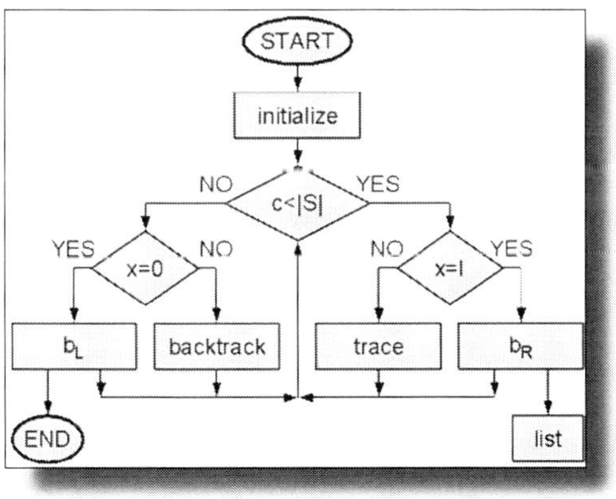

alpha test...

In-house testing that happens before the product is supposed to be sold in order to discover any problems that the product may have.

amend...

To change or improve something. Think of the Amendments to the *U.S. Constitution*.

assembly line...

A method of production in which one thing is done at a time, before it's passed along for the next step, in order to be more efficient.

average cost curve (short & long term)...

A graph that shows how much a product has cost over a long term or short-term period.

bells and whistles...

Fancy additions to something. A car has all the 'bells and whistles' if it has a sunroof, heated seats, a navigation system, satellite radio, etc.

benchmark...

A guideline or standard used in order to measure quality, value, or success in order to make any changes.

best practice...

The best and most efficient process that has proved to be much better than all the others. Finding the fastest road to a destination would be the best practice for that driving situation.

beta test...

Testing a product by having groups try it out in order to see what problems, if any, occur during normal use that other tests may have missed. Mozilla Firefox, along with many other software programs, usually have a beta version in order to find any bugs that were not spotted earlier.

blueprint...

A plan, generally drawn out, for the construction of a building.

brainstorming...

A way of coming up with new ideas that typically uses creative methods by a group.

breakthrough product...

Any type of product or good that is new, fresh, and changes the market in some way because of how different it is from everything else, like when the first video games on the market changed how people, particularly children and teenagers, spent their free time.

building blocks...

The basics of anything, or a starting point. Think back to when you used to play with LEGO or any other sort of block as a kid. All of the later bricks depended on the first 'bricks' that you put down and how you placed them.

CAD (computer aided design)...

A way of designing ideas that uses computers to help make an accurate visual for a new idea.

CAM (computer assisted manufacturing)...

The use of computers to make a product. This usually is a faster, more efficient, and sometimes safer way of manufacturing because the computers are in control of the machines that make the product.

come on line...

When a product or service becomes active and is ready to be used or sold.

defect...

Some problem or issue with a product that causes it to work less properly than it should. If your new computer won't turn on or charge the battery, then it has a defect of some sort.

develop...

When someone has created a snazzy new product or made changes (and hopefully improvements) on a current one. A product can be developed and redeveloped as many times as the manufacturer thinks is needed. For a great example of this, think of the many changes made to any Apple or Microsoft product as technology has improved.

ECV (expected commercial value)...

How much worth something is believed to have once it's released out on the market.

feasibility review/study...

A study of a project or venture to determine its true strengths and weaknesses, the resources needed, and the opportunities or threats that arise from its creation.

gamma test...

The testing that follows beta tests and occurs before the product is to go to the market.

high-speed...

Regarding technology, this is the faster speed of what's around today in comparison older versions. Today's high-speed anything is tomorrow's "you gotta be kidding!"

import/export...

An import is something that you get from another source, while an export is something you give to another source. Think of how we get most of our gasoline from other countries (meaning it's imported to us and exported from them).

innovation...

The design and development of new ideas and products. Many companies have an entire team dedicated to this, like finding new ways to make smart phones even smarter.

inspection...

An examination or check-up of something in order to make sure that everything is going as well as it should. When restaurants are inspected, the government is making sure that these places are doing everything to make their food and location safe for the public.

lifecycles of products...

The stages of how producst go from being fresh and new to being old and/or outdated throughout development, production, and while on the market.

logistics...

The planning, maintenance, organization, and distribution of goods and services in order to get such goods and services from the state of production to a state of consumption.

market opportunity...

The chance to sell a good, service, or product somewhere that someone else isn't already selling.

market share...

How much of a product one company sells in a certain part of the market at a certain time. This would be like calculating how many shoes Nike sells versus any other company.

market test...

A way of finding out if a new product would interest consumers before actually putting the product on the market.

mass production...

The creation of lots of the same product in one given time and/or place.

mindmapping...

Some sort of visual illustration of a bunch of connected ideas. Think of a spider web, but with ideas instead of bugs.

obsolescence...

To turn obsolete, or no longer wanted or needed, generally because something new, better, and/or faster has taken its place. If you've ever seen or if your parents ever owned a VHS or VCR, then you probably know that they've become obsolete since DVD players have become more popular and efficient.

PAC (project approval committee)...

...But not PAC man! This is the group of people who decide whether or not a product is worthy of being created or ready to go to market after it has been created.

paradigm...

A pattern or model of something.

phase review...

An overview of work results on a particular section of a project or product. The results of this review will determine if you will move on to the next phase or portion of the project.

product development process...

How a product goes from an idea, to production, to market. For example, the process of developing a new type of technology is probably a long one.

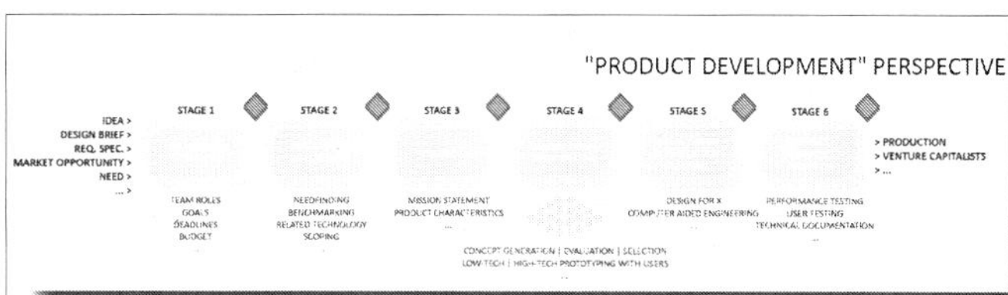

PIDs (products in development)...

Products being created and produced.

PIMs (products in market)...

Products being sold.

prototype...

An early product sample or model built to test a new concept, design, or process.

quality control...

The guidelines and rules set to make sure that everything is done in a consistent manner, like product production, customer service, etc. This helps to make sure that your new car gets further than the driveway!

quota...

A desired or set limit of a number of something.

reengineer...

This is when major changes are made within the structure of a company or in how things are done.

reverse engineering...

Taking apart a competitor's product so you can learn everything about it, usually for the purpose of copying their product.

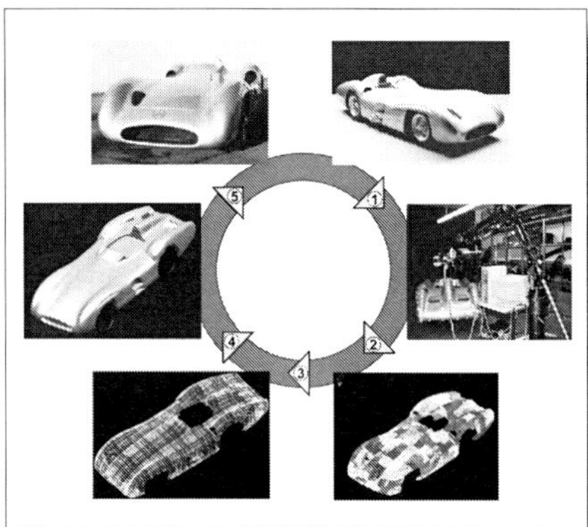

rolling launch...

The slow introduction of a new product, like when a movie first opens in select theatres before it opens nationwide.

seamless integration...

The introduction of something new that works with the existing system without interruption. For example, when businesses and websites began using Facebook and other social media in order to connect with consumers.

skunkworks...

This describes a product development program that is kept outside the normal procedure in order to keep it secret.

streamline...

The process of making something more efficient and productive. For example, the latest cell phones have made communication much easier and faster than it was in the past.

template...

Something used to model all other products or ideas. Microsoft Word has different templates in order to make different types of documents, like calendars or invitations.

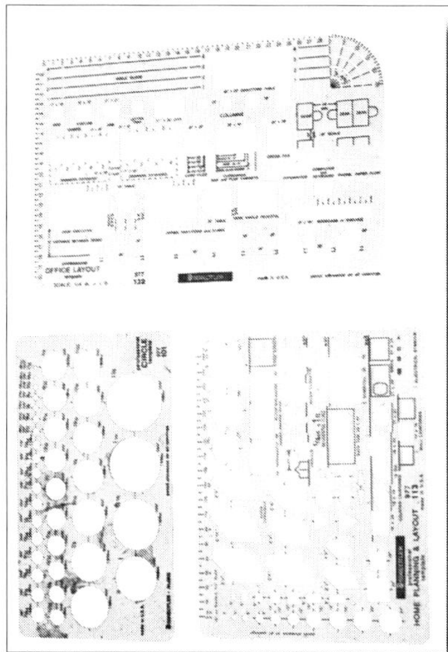

widget...

A name for any hypothetical manufactured product that has yet to be made.

zilch!...

Zero error rate; the number of errors most businesses shoot for in any process or operation.

Marketing • Advertising

"above the fold"...

In graphic design, this is the premiere placement of a story or a photograph on the upper half of the front page of a website or newspaper. This designation indicates that the story or photograph is the most important item to be viewed.

audience...

The group that will see, hear, read, or in some other way come into contact with your message or product.

banner ad...

An ad that goes across the top and sometimes bottom of a webpage that advertises a certain good or service. Many websites have these to help pay for the costs of running the website.

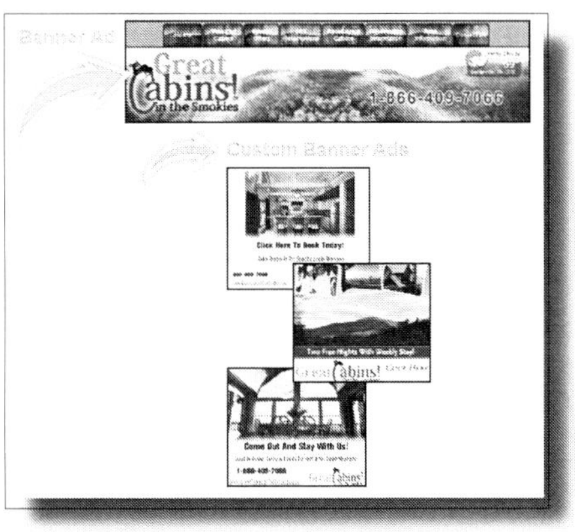

brand...

The particular company logo or image that a consumer associates with a specific product. This can be anything from Apple's iProducts to McDonald's McAnything.

brand association...

Images and symbols that are associated with a particular brand, such as McDonald's Golden Arches, Coke's contoured bottle, or the Nike Swoosh!

brand loyalty...

The tendency for consumers to consistently buy products from the same manufacturer with no regard for the same product from other manufacturer. Are you a Coke drinker or a Pepsi drinker?

brand share...

The amount of money consumers spend on one particular brand vs. the other competitive brands.

buzzword...

An important term specific to a certain field or group. For instance, the book you are currently reading is filled with Business, Work, and Career-related buzzwords!

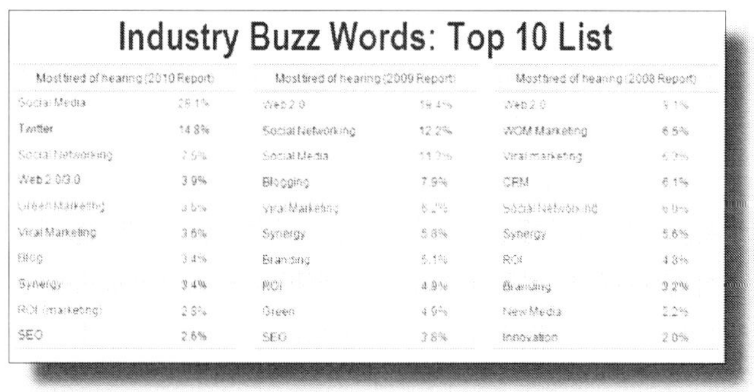

Industry Buzz Words: Top 10 List

Most tired of hearing (2010 Report)		Most tired of hearing (2009 Report)		Most tired of hearing (2008 Report)	
Social Media	28.1%	Web 2.0	19.4%	Web 2.0	9.1%
Twitter	14.8%	Social Networking	12.2%	WOM Marketing	6.5%
Social Networking	7.5%	Social Media	11.7%	Viral marketing	6.3%
Web 2.0/3.0	3.9%	Blogging	7.9%	CRM	6.1%
Green Marketing	3.6%	Viral Marketing	6.2%	Social Networking	6.0%
Viral Marketing	3.6%	Synergy	5.8%	Synergy	5.6%
Blog	3.4%	Branding	5.1%	ROI	4.8%
Synergy	3.4%	ROI	4.9%	Branding	3.2%
ROI (marketing)	2.8%	Green	4.9%	New Media	2.2%
SEO	2.6%	SEO	3.8%	Innovation	2.0%

campaign...

A planned set of actions designed to reach an objective. In marketing, different campaigns are made to market and sell different products.

circulation...

How many people a publication reaches on average. In print, for example, this is how many copies are printed and given out in a certain period.

classified ad...

An announcement in a newspaper, magazine, or on a website that is organized into different categories, including Employment Opportunities, Services, and Pets, among others. This means that in one page, you could find a job, a house, a car, and a dog! How crazy is that?

co-op advertising...

The agreement between a manufacturer and a distributor to share the cost of advertising. For example, a cereal manufacturer and a grocery store may split the cost of advertising for a big cereal sale—bringing more shoppers to the grocery store and more cereal buyers. It is beneficial to both!

demographics...

This uses statistics in order to group people by some sort of similar feature, like age, gender, income etc. This can be useful knowledge in advertising because the advertisers can make sure their product reaches the right group or audience.

double-page spread...

In print media, like in a book or magazine, when an advertisement, photo, or article takes up two pages facing each other.

email blast...

A way of marketing using electronic communication (emails).

feature...

Not like brown eyes or button nose. This is an article or story in a magazine, newspaper, radio, or television news program that focuses on topic and goes into detail. It can be on anything from recycling to the life and times of your favorite celebrity.

focus group...

A group of people brought together to give their opinions on a particular product, usually for marketing research.

info-graphic...

Graphic, visual representations of information, data, or knowledge. Consider using info-graphics on your resume to better show information about you.

mailing list...

A list of names and contact information that is used to advertise a product or service. The persons or businesses on a mailing list is the target of an advertising campaign.

market research...

Before a product can be sold, some research must be done on other similar products, the consumers, and ways in which the consumer can buy the product. This information, called market research, must be gathered and analyzed to produce the most effective and appropriate information for the manufacturer or developer. This helps to ensure that a certain product reaches a consumer that would be most interested in it.

metadata...

Data about data! Metadata is description of data within an electronic document used to help sort, optimize, and search for specific documents or other data.

objective/subjective...

Objective viewpoint ignores someone's likes or personal opinions. Subjective viewpoint depends entirely on someone's likes or personal opinions, like if I think that chocolate is the best dessert ever because it's my favorite.

off the record/on the record...

In journalism, "off the record" is the gathering of confidential information from confidential sources. "On the record" is gathering timely, official information from public, named sources.

pagination...

The system in which pages are separated and numbered in a document, either electronic or printed.

peer-to-peer...

Also known as P2P. It's a marketing strategy that encourages customers to attract other customers. When your credit card company offers you an incentive get a friend to sign up, they are using a P2P marketing strategy.

press kit...

Information sent to the media that explains what a company does and sells. This is a good way of getting a company's name and products out to the public.

press release...

A statement released in the media that announces news about a company, product, or person.

product launch...

The introduction of a new product using media and advertisements in order to get the word out to the public about the new or improved product, like when you see a bunch of commercials for an awesome new weight loss gadget!

public relations...

The use of media in order to ensure the person, group, company, or product maintains a good public image even when something has occurred that may tarnish that image. This is different from advertising in many ways, one of which is the company does not purchase the public relations article, whereas they would purchase the advertisement.

search engine optimization (SEO)...

Making the most of pages like Google, Bing, and Yahoo to help people find your website after a search, by making the site a top result.

slogan...

A catchy phrase used in advertisements that sums up a product or company and tries to make customers remember it, like Wendy's "You Know When It's Real" line.

social media...

Sites like Facebook, Twitter, and LinkedIn, which people use in order to connect with other people through messages, pictures, or whatever the site specializes in.

spin (as in media spin)...

How the media presents information to the public. This can be like trying to make something bad seem positive, especially when a company or celebrity says or does something that they shouldn't.

sponsor...

A company or firm that in some way supports, either financially or through special gifts, a team, school, or other such organization in exchange for an assurance of advertisement opportunities. For example, many school sports teams have sponsors that help with the costs of the team in exchange for some sort of advertising at the game.

target audience...

A certain group of people that an advertisement hopes to reach, like athletes for a PowerAde commercial.

value-added...

An improvement that a business makes to a product in order to give it an edge over other similar and possibly identical products. An example of this is a warranty on your computer, iPod, or car. Even your messaging and data plan with your cell phone is considered a value-added service!

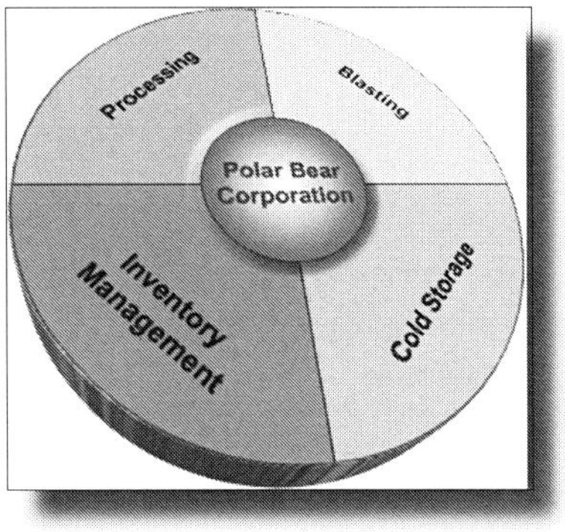

vertical vs. horizontal...

Vertical market is a group of similar businesses and customers with similar needs, and in a similar industry. For example, surgical instrument manufacturers create products for hospitals only. Horizontal market is a group of businesses and customers that share needs that span across many or all industries. For example, car manufacturers create cars for individuals, businesses, government, etc.

whitepaper...

An authoritative report or guide to help its readers understand an issue, solve a problem, or make a decision. Whitepapers can be great marketing materials for a company to send its customers to keep them updated on industry trends or product information.

word-of-mouth advertising...

A free type of advertising that relies on customers to tell people that they know about the good or service, like after I tell you and everyone else I know that Happy Hamburgers has the best burgers in the entire universe and you go try one and then tell all of your friends. Don't you think we should get a free fry or two for all this free publicity?

LIGHTS... CAMERA... ACTION!

You have snagged your first real job—congrats! Now, get to work!

After you fill-out your **W-2** form with all the information about your **dependents**(?!), **deductions**, and such (are you **exempt,** or **non-exempt**?), it will be time for your first **staff meeting**. Your **priorities** will certainly each have **deadlines**. You may want to set up a **"tickler file"** to remind you of these. **Accountability** is key in a new job!

Your **job description** and the **employee manual** will guide you, as will your new **supervisor** to whom you will be a **direct report**. (That's not paper, fyi!) Perhaps your new company uses the **lean** method. If so, you'll certainly care about **kaizen**, right? (You know: **quality control**, **quality assurance**, **continuous improvement**, and all that jazz!)

Hmm, seems there are a lot of **new-hires** today. Hope you all pick up on the **corporate culture** quickly and don't get caught up in **office politics** too soon. After all, you have a lot of work to do!

What? When is "break?" Hahahahahaha!

Meetings • Presentations • Communications

attachment...

A computer file that rides along with an email message. Attachments are used universally to send documents, photos, graphics, videos, music, etc. between users.

attention line...

The line in a formal letter that says specifically whom the letter is for within a company. For example, if you were writing to a Patsy Harbin, who works for Totally Technological, Inc., then you include the 'Attention' line in the company address.

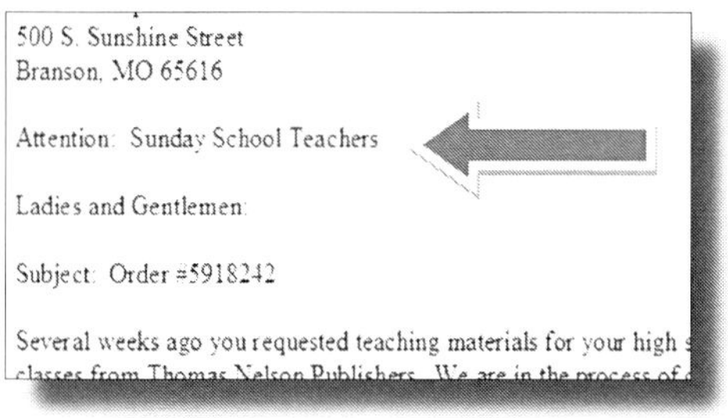
500 S. Sunshine Street
Branson, MO 65616

Attention: Sunday School Teachers

Ladies and Gentlemen:

Subject: Order #5918242

Several weeks ago you requested teaching materials for your high

bargaining...

A negotiation between two parties when terms can't be agreed upon.

blind copy (BCC)...

In emails, this is when you send a copy of an email to someone, but everyone else who receives the email can't see that person's information. For example, you can send an email to yourself and then put your list of recipients in the blind copy category in order to protect their privacy.

body language...

A type of communication that uses body movements, gestures, and placements rather than words to describe how a person is feeling.

conference call...

A business call including more than two people, generally all in separate locations.

enclosure...

An enclosure is a hard copy or tangible item that rides along with a cover letter or memo, and to keep them together, they are enclosed within an envelope or folder.

feature...

Not a facial feature. An article or story in a magazine, newspaper, or other type of medium that focuses on a main subject.

flip chart...

A large pad of paper that a person uses for a presentation.

letterhead...

A piece of stationery or other nice paper that has the company's logo or name at the top and indicates an official company letter. If your school principal has ever sent out an official letter, then it was probably on the school letterhead.

memorandum (memo)...

A short document or note sent within the company. This would be like if your mom left you a note saying you needed to take out the trash.

minutes...

In business, this has nothing to do with your cell phone plan. These are the notes taken at a meeting, detailing all the major points discussed. If you've ever gone to a meeting for a club at school, then someone has probably taken notes at the meeting so what you talked about won't be forgotten for the next one!

need-to-know...

Only receiving information or knowledge when it is absolutely essential. Sometimes managers share information with employees on a "need-to-know" basis.

negotiation...

The give and take between two parties who may have some sort of conflict. In the business world, this could be between the employer and the employee for the employee's salary.

pie chart...

A circular graph depicting quantities. It is divided into sections based on amounts—similar to slices of a pie!

radar chart (spider chart)...

A graphic way of analyzing data that uses lines emanating from the same point. If charting multiple variables, the chart looks like a spider's web.

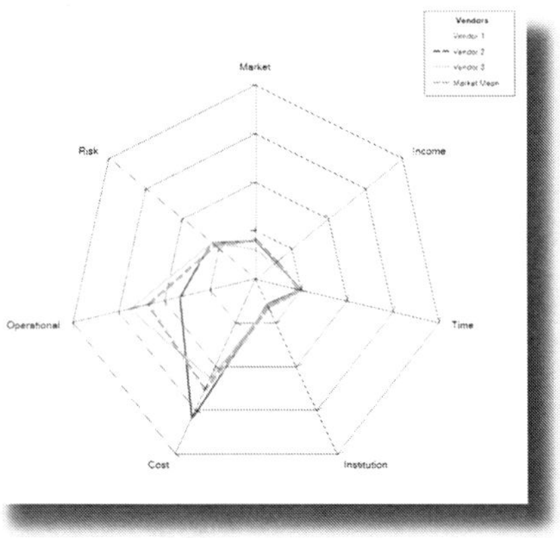

ultimatum...

This is a tough decision that is forced on someone where neither option is good for the person making the decision. For example, if you have been given a difficult assignment to do overnight and your teacher tells you that you must finish it for the next class or else fail, you've been given an ultimatum!

visual aid...

Any sort of poster, graph, diagram, slideshow, image, video, or other medium that helps visualize the presenter's idea in a presentation.

webinar...

A live presentation or workshop conducted, transmitted, and viewed online. Participants can take part in the presentation and ask questions. Webinars disseminate information firsthand without the cost of transporting participants to a central location. They can be used for any purpose. A national restaurant chain just used a webinar to train all of their cooks to make the newest dish on the menu.

Miscellaneous Work Words

acquisition...

The process of buying the assets and operations of another company to strengthen and grow the acquiring company.

ad hoc...

A fancy Latin term referring to something that has a specific purpose for a specific time and place, such as an ad hoc committee.

allocate...

To set aside something for a specific purpose, such as designating funds to purchase office equipment.

analyze/evaluate/synthesize...

Things you might be expected to do with data in order to quantify value, compare differences, project future results, and make decisions.

assignment...

A task given to a certain person or group, usually with guidelines and a due date.

big picture...

The grand scheme, the whole idea.

bottom-line...

A company's net earnings or income. A company "improving its bottom-line" is growing net earnings and reducing costs.

business opportunity...

A chance (of investment) to either go into business or make a business deal that has the ability of being successful, like when your friend decides to start a t-shirt business and asks for help to pay for supplies in exchange for part of future profits.

butterfly effect...

The idea that one small action or choice can make a huge impact on everything that follows it. It refers to the idea that if a butterfly flaps its wings in Africa and moves air, eventually there will be a tornado somewhere else.

by-product...

Something produced as a result of making something else. This can be something tangible made while creating a product or even knowledge learned in the course of doing business.

by the book...

Following the rules, taking the safer route. There are loads of examples of people on TV who don't go 'by the book' in their jobs.

change agent...

Someone who is hired by a business to assist the employees though an organizational change or transition.

chaos...

From order to disorder. When small events and changes lead to a huge, random mess, chaos has arrived.

closure...

When something comes to an end.

convergence...

When differences come together and meet at a common point. They can also lose some of what makes them different and become more similar to each other after convergence has happened.

data...

Information, facts, details, notes, reports, observations, evidence, measurements, statistics, scores, conclusions, experiments, materials, knowledge, research, figures, input, memos, pictures...shall I go on?

deadline...

A due date for a project, report, communication, or goal. To be successful in your career, this is NOT something you want to miss—no matter what!

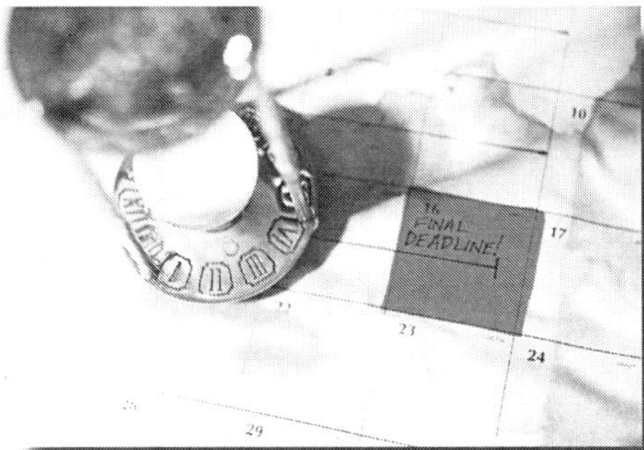

delegating...

Breaking a task apart into smaller, more manageable steps and assigning those steps to separate people to complete. A manager may delegate tasks to her staff.

execution...

Performing an action, such as signing a contract.

exit strategy...

Like the name says, this is a plan that a person, group, or company has in order to leave a situation either after a positive end has been reached or before something negative happens.

facilitate...

To help a person complete his task, or help an assignment to achieve completion. Basically, to help anyone do anything.

goodwill...

A really beneficial relationship a business can have with its customers and community.

implementation...

When you take a plan from the thinking stage to the doing stage.

interconnectedness...

When two or more things connect and relate to one another in an attempt to achieve a goal.

logic-based...

Using your head to make decisions and carry out tasks, and not your heart or emotions. Essential to be successful in the business world.

logistics...

The plan for how materials get where they need to go when they need to be there.

maintenance...

Caring for and managing equipment, systems, or operations.

metrics...

A means of measuring intangible things, like efficiency, progress, and performance.

middleman...

A person who represents someone else in business arrangements or connects people who want to work together. They usually are paid for their work from a percentage of the money earned by the business transaction.

minimum performance requirements...

The most basic parts of an act or product that are considered acceptable.

niche...

A place or specialty in which things flourish. A frog's niche can be a certain pond, or a business's niche could be selling a particular product or marketing to a particular audience.

outcome...

Something that follows as a result or consequence. Could be positive or negative; could be expected or surprising.

overhaul...

To inspect or examine a product or process in order to change or revise it.

pace of change...

How fast a situation changes within a business.

per se...

Huh? It's a Latin term for "in or by itself." "I don't know that his success is due to only luck per se – his talent and professionalism also probably had something to do with it."

policy...

A plan of action or formal procedure used to conduct business. A business will have set policies all employees are expected to follow.

process...

A series of actions, tasks, or functions that are followed to produce a desired result. Establishing an efficient process to create a product is important. Every member of a team or business should follow the same steps to achieve the same result.

quid pro quo...

What goes around comes around. Getting something for something. If you give something valuable, you'll get something valuable. If you give something negative, you'll get something negative in return.

red herring...

Something that draws attention away from the true issue.

requisition...

A formal written request for something that is needed.

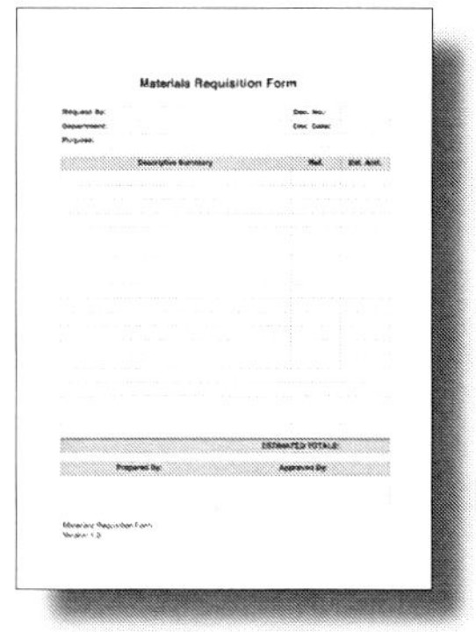

response time...

The length of time it takes to respond.

retroactive...

Putting a policy into effect based on a date in the past. If you receive a retroactive raise, you will receive back pay based on a previous date and going forward into the future.

social responsibility...

The idea that a company should try to do more good than harm when it comes to anything affecting the public, like supporting a charity or not polluting the drinking water supply.

sustainable...

The ability to endure or to be upheld over time.

task vs. process...

The task is the end goal, assignment, or product, like completing a proposal, and the process is all the steps you take to get to that goal!

top down/bottom up...

A way of looking at things, either from large overview to detailed, small facts (top-down), or from small particulars to large generalities (bottom-up).

transition...

Going through a change in the way business is conducted.

unilateral...

Recognizing an issue or making a decision after consideration of only one side of a subject. A CEO is within her right to make a unilateral decision about her business if she thinks it is the right thing to do.

upfront...

When money is paid out at the beginning of a business transaction.

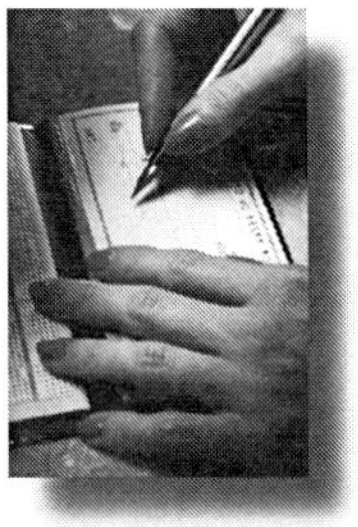

walk the walk/talk the talk...

A phrase used when you need to completely assume an identity. If you become a manager, you'll need to walk the walk and talk the talk, meaning you'll need to act like a manager in every way.

zero defects...

When there are no problems in a product or process.

Newfangled...

Newfangled work words come on board all the time. To keep up with them, read the latest hot-topic business books. No time? Then at least read their titles and learn what these new terms mean! They may become part of the water cooler talk around the office, and you sure don't want to sound old-fogey and out of the loop, right?

Just for starters, go forth and learn the meaning of:
(Hint: They all have one thing in common!)

outlier
tipping point
blink
lean
art of execution

fast company
strategic selling
perfect pitch
power listening
all business is local

wealth of nations
world is flat
fifth discipline
e-myth
good to great

(Each word or term is the title or part of the title of a bestselling business book!)

Personal Skills

adapt to change...

Being able to take changes in stride and make then into a positive situation.

administrative skills...

A set of abilities that is useful and necessary to work in Administration. These skills can include experience working with phones, computers, and customers and being well organized and able to communicate, among others.

common sense...

The knowledge of things you can't really learn in books. Plain ordinary good judgement.

detail-oriented...

Paying close attention to detail in everything.

ethics...

Principles, morals, something to live and work by–these are a sort of code that can help keep people out of trouble should they follow them. Examples are not cheating or stealing.

etiquette...

The proper or best way of acting, dressing, and speaking, particularly with good manners. Etiquette is extremely vital during a job interview, as first impressions are always important.

generalist...

The opposite of a specialist, this is someone who knows about several different things. This would be your regular family doctor, rather than a pediatrician or cardiologist.

goal setting...

As the name says, this is finding some sort of end point that you want to reach by a certain time, like selling $4,000.00 in ads by month end.

good-faith...

Acting with honest intentions, without intent to trick or deceive others.

individual growth plan...

This is a plan that charts your career path, letting you know what you need to learn when, and how to achieve your career goals.

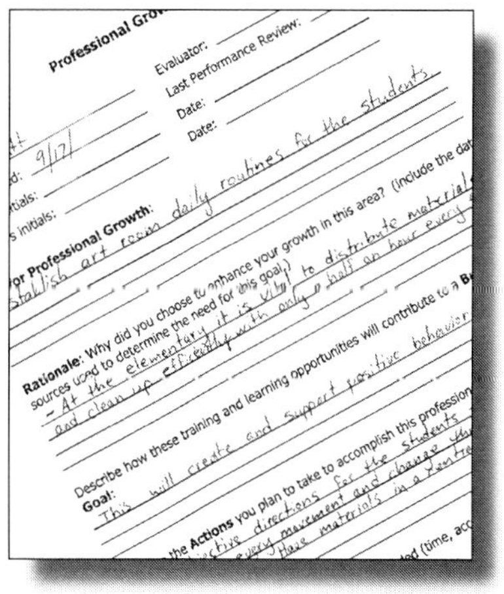

initiative-taking...

When someone does things on their own without being told or waiting for instruction. This person is a self-motivated doer.

know-how...

This is the knowledge of how to do something, like computer know-how–the skill or ability to work well with computers.

knowledge worker...

Workers who are required to "think" for a living, such as software engineers or lawyers.

lifelong learning...

Pursuing knowledge throughout your life for self-motivated reasons, be they personal or professional.

motivation...

What makes you work as hard (or not) as you can to achieve a goal?

productivity...

The measure of how efficient you are when doing your work. Workers with high productivity ignore distractions, use their time wisely, and focus on the task at hand.

results-oriented...

Always keeping the end result in mind in order to achieve the best possible one.

self-direction...

Being able to work independently without having someone tell you what you need to do every few minutes.

self-motivated...

When someone does not need outside inspiration to start a job or work his hardest.

self-sufficiency...

Being able to rely on youself for what you need instead of constantly needing someone else to help out.

soft (essential) skills...

These skills are more about who you are and how you deal with things, rather than what you know and what you can do. Examples are being on time, dressing appropriately, and using good manners.

specialist...

Someone who focuses on something specific. A cardiologist, for example, is a doctor who specializes in the human heart.

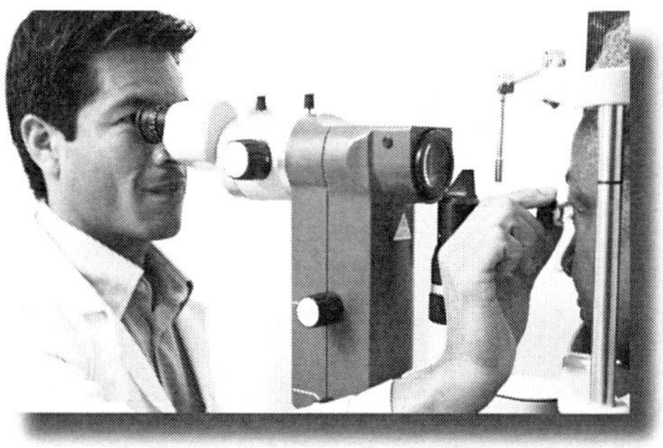

talent...

A group of dependable, skilled workers that can be called on to do a required task.

Sales

agreement of sale...

An official, legal deal ensuring that the good will be bought and sold according to the agreement, like when you're buying a car or house.

air freight...

The transportation of goods or products through the air by using some sort of airplane. UPS sometimes uses this in order to ship packages.

as is...

Selling a product in its current state to a consumer, with any problems that it may already have. Some people buy cars 'as is,' meaning that they are responsible for any repairs needed after they have purchased it.

asking price...

The amount of money that the seller wants for their product.

bid...

To offer to buy a product or service at a particular price. The seller can accept or decline the bid, or negotiate a price with the buyer so both parties are happy.

black market...

The sale of illegal goods, like stolen televisions.

branch...

But not the kind hanging off of trees. This is a specific location of a store or office.

buy out...

To purchase the entire stock of inventory, or to purchase the entire rights to a business.

buy-back agreement...

To make an arrangement to purchase something that has previously been sold, lost, or given away.

buyer's market...

Market conditions when it's better to be buying than selling ... meaning that prices are lower, usually because there is a surplus of the goods.

cold call...

An unexpected attempt at a sale, either through a visit or a call to a new, potential customer. Telemarketers are an example of this, as you never know when they'll call you!

commission...

A payment to employees based on sales and work performance that is in addition to, or sometimes instead of, a base salary. Earning commissions is a motivation for employees to work hard to close sales for their business or company. Commissions tend to be a percentage of sales that are usually based on the amount of work necessary to close a sale.

customer...

The person who really signs your paycheck! If the customer doesn't buy your product or service, then your company won't have the money to pay YOU!

fulfillment...

In businesses that mail the product to the buyer, this is the completion of 'filling' that order, or of packing and shipping it to the customer. So after you buy a handy new blanket from Amazon.com, once they have processed, packed, and shipped your blanket, they have fulfilled your order.

hard sell...

An aggressive, insistent, in-your-face sales pitch. A good example: you walk in to a car dealership and a salesman walks up to you and asks "What can I do to put you into a new car right now?"

inside sales...

Selling products or services via phone or email, not meeting with customers face to face. Inside sales representatives usually conduct cold calls to gain new customers or call current client lists to gain additional business.

inventory...

The count of all goods in stock.

kiosks...

A small place, like a booth or cart rather than an actual store, for goods to be sold in a mall or other similar public area. If you're ever been to a mall, then you've more than likely seen many of these, in the middle of the walkway, selling phones and accessories.

mark up...

To increase the price of a product or service in order to cover production costs and add a margin of profit.

metrics...

Measurement of the amount of something—goods sold, dollars earned, expenses spent, etc.

outbid...

To offer more money to purchase a product or service than someone else who also wants to purchase that product or service.

outside sales...

Selling products or services by leaving the office and meeting with customers or potential customers face to face. Though initial meetings with customers might be made over the phone, outside sales representatives will attempt to close the deal in person.

point of sale...

The physical location where a product is sold to the consumer, like at your favorite neighborhood store or online marketplace.

point of sale (POS) system...

A type of computer software that allows the tracking of inventory and sales through many checkout counters.

products and services...

The basis of all business. All businesses either MAKE something for their customers (products) or DO something for their customers (services).

prospects (sales prospects)...

In business, this refers to someone who could possibly become a customer.

retail...

The sale of goods directly to consumers.

soft sell...

A subtle, friendly, or casual sale pitch. A good example: you watch a hilarious viral video on the Internet that brings attention to a product and because of the video, you go out and buy that product.

stock...

The supply of a product for sale in a store. For example, after Valentine's Day, Wal-Mart has a sale on its remaining stock of Valentine's candy.

transaction...

An agreement in business between two people, companies, or groups, where one gives some sort of service in exchange for money or another service.

vendor...

A person or entity that sells a product.

warranty...

A promise to the consumer that a product, good, or service will be up to a certain set of standards for a certain amount of time or else the consumer will receive some sort of benefit, like a replacement or their money back. Cars, refrigerators, and other sorts of technology come with a warranty with a certain time frame. These warranties help assure the customer that they will not find fault with their usually expensive purchase, but if they do, all hope is not lost.

wholesale...

The sale of a product in large numbers. Sam's Club, Costco, and BJ's are all examples of wholesale stores.

PROFIT: the amount left, if any, from a company's revenues after all expenses and taxes are paid

Question: How much profit (percentagewise) do you think the average company makes on every dollar it takes in?

Answer: 5%

When Things Go Wrong at Work

blacklist...

A list of businesses or businesspeople that are considered disreputable or unreliable...or someone who is denied work in a particular field because of something bad in their previous work history.

boondoggle...

A scheme that wastes time and money. If a business project is overbudget, behind schedule, or even completely unnecessary, it is considered a boondoggle.

conflict...

When two people don't work together well or have incompatible ways of doing work. It is not uncommon to have conflict with someone you work with, but it is essential that you learn to compromise so that business can be completed.

demotion...

A reduction or downgrade in position or status. A demotion may also mean a reduction in salary or pay.

downsize...

When a company lets employees go in order to cut expenses and save money.

furlough...

A temporary layoff from work. Sometimes businesses will temporarily lay off employees during low production time periods.

GIGO...

Garbage in, garbage out. The rule that the quality of output is the same as the quality of input. If you use sloppy techniques or poor quality parts to produce a widget, then the widget will also be sloppy and poor quality.

garnishment...

A legal order allowing an official entity to take money that is owed to you as payment for a debt that you owe to that entity. If you fail to pay taxes to the U.S. Government, the IRS can garnish your wages to pay those taxes.

glut...

An excess of goods in the market so that supply outweighs demand for those goods. The value of those goods then falls.

goldbrick...

To avoid or neglect doing your job.

golden parachute...

An agreement between a company and a senior executive saying that even if the executive is fired or if the company is taken over for some reason, the executive will still receive a substantial income or other benefits.

kickback...

A form of bribery...paying someone or some entity to ignore illegal activity. Or giving someone business or money that is not ethically earned.

malpractice...

Negligence or misconduct by a professional worker, such as a doctor or lawyer.

nepotism...

To show favoritism, preferential treatment, or give unfair advantage to a family member.

not invented here (NIH)...

Sometimes someone may put down a very good idea you have, not because it's not a good idea, but because it was "Not Invented Here" if you brought that idea in from outside. Never stick your nose in the air at any good idea, no matter where it came from. That's silly.

picket line...

Employees marching in front of a business while on strike to protest or publicize disagreement with something the business is doing.

pink slip...

If you receive a pink slip, you've been fired from your job.

Ponzi scheme...

Investment fraud in which a businessman takes money from investors and instead of actually investing that money, he keeps it for his own benefit. The businessman then must get money from new investors to pay off the old investors. Ever heard of Bernie Madoff?

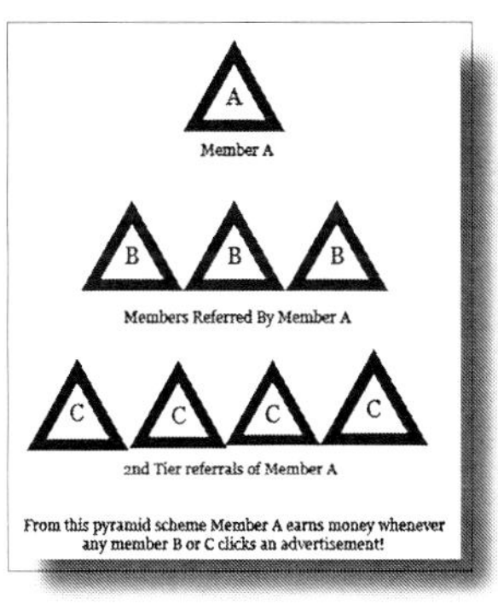

punitive measures...

Punishment of an individual or organization for their actions.

push back...

This term can refer either to resistance to an idea or plan, or having to move a deadline to a later date.

red tape...

Rules and bureaucracy of a government or large corporation that actually hinders good business actions or decisions instead of helps.

scandal...

Most businesses or business people are involved in a "scandal" when they do wrong. There is never any free lunch; when you do bad it always comes back to haunt you. Always be above board and honest...it pays off in the long run. Your reputation is a precious thing!

strike...

When employees stop working for a period of time to protest unfair working conditions or demand better pay.

unethical...

Actions that are not conforming to the approved standards of social or professional behavior.

vote of no confidence...

At work, if your peers begin to feel you are not a committed part of the team, are not capable, or are slacking off and leaving them to do the heavy lifting, you may find yourself ostracized, say not receiving emails or memos or being invited to meetings. You might say they are giving you a "vote of no confidence."

whistle-blower...

Someone who exposes some sort of wrongdoing in a business.

RESUME: a one-page sheet of your educational accomplishments, achievments and awards, and work experience; it does not have to be boring!

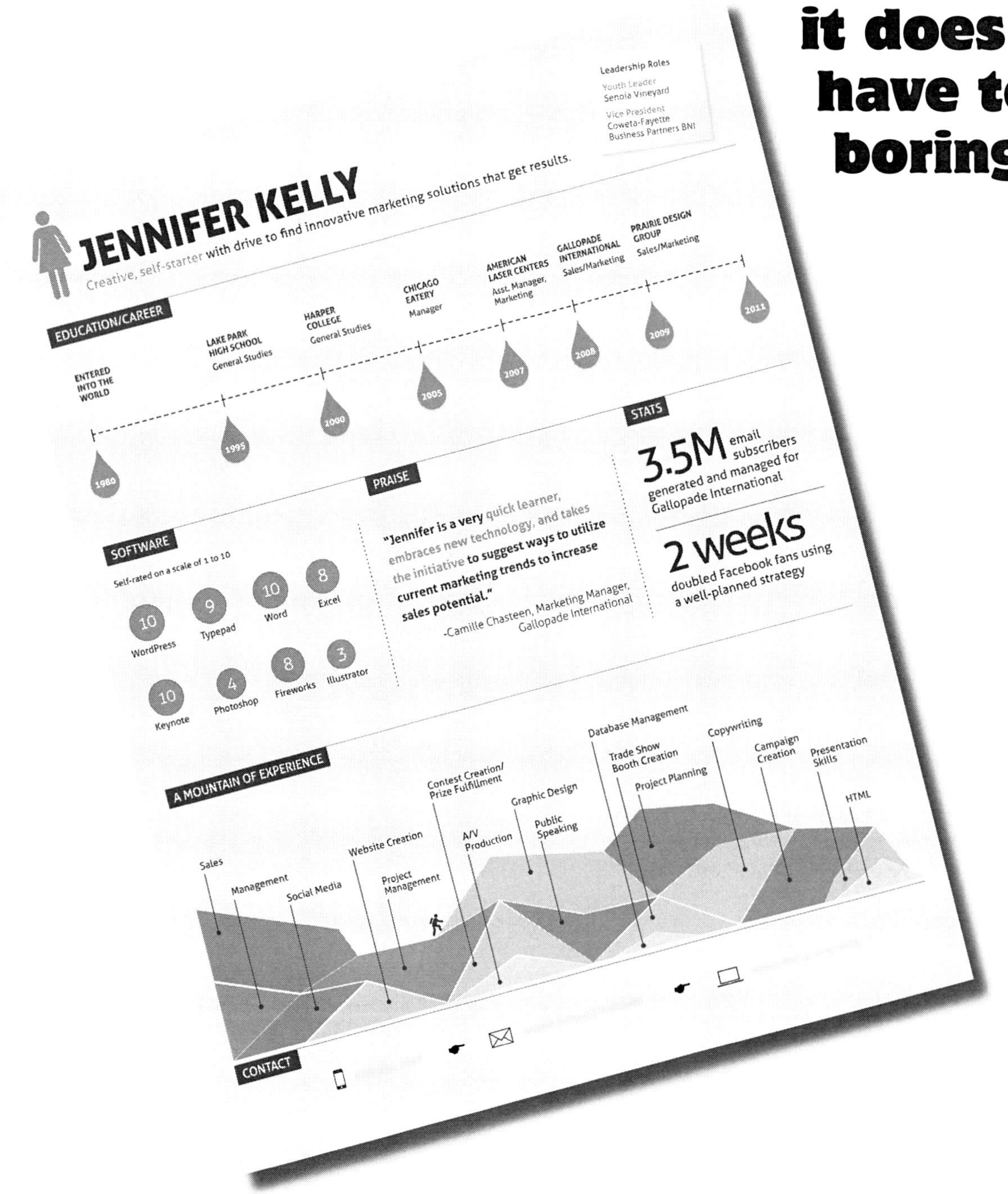
Leadership Roles
Youth Leader
Senoia Vineyard
Vice President
Coweta-Fayette
Business Partners BNI

JENNIFER KELLY
Creative, self-starter with drive to find innovative marketing solutions that get results.

EDUCATION/CAREER
ENTERED INTO THE WORLD — 1980
LAKE PARK HIGH SCHOOL General Studies — 1995
HARPER COLLEGE General Studies — 2000
CHICAGO EATERY Manager — 2005
AMERICAN LASER CENTERS Asst. Manager, Marketing — 2007
GALLOPADE INTERNATIONAL Sales/Marketing — 2008
PRAIRIE DESIGN GROUP Sales/Marketing — 2009
2011

STATS
3.5M email subscribers generated and managed for Gallopade International
2 weeks doubled Facebook fans using a well-planned strategy

PRAISE
"Jennifer is a very quick learner, embraces new technology, and takes the initiative to suggest ways to utilize current marketing trends to increase sales potential."
-Camille Chasteen, Marketing Manager, Gallopade International

SOFTWARE
Self-rated on a scale of 1 to 10
10 WordPress
9 Typepad
10 Word
8 Excel
10 Keynote
4 Photoshop
8 Fireworks
3 Illustrator

A MOUNTAIN OF EXPERIENCE
Sales
Management
Social Media
Website Creation
Project Management
Contest Creation/ Prize Fulfillment
A/V Production
Graphic Design
Public Speaking
Database Management
Trade Show Booth Creation
Project Planning
Copywriting
Campaign Creation
Presentation Skills
HTML

CONTACT

Business Names & Places to Know

Big Business...

A symbolic term describing large corporations such as Exxon, Microsoft, Google, or WalMart. Activities carried out by "big business" affect entire industries and economies.

Bill...

Bill Gates, of Microsoft and Windows fame.

Jim Collins...

The author of *Good to Great*, a best-selling book well-admired for its advice on how to make a business successful.

Stephen Covey...

The author of the bestseller *Seven Habits of Highly Effective People* and all the similar sequels to it.

Peter Drucker...

An influential writer about of management theory books and articles. He actually coined the term "knowledge worker."

The Fed...

The Federal Reserve Board; when they speak, everyone listens, especially when they change the prime rate up or down, or even keep it the same.

Michael Dell...

Another digital guru, creator of Dell Computers.

movers and shakers...

People who are active, knowledgeable, influential in a particular field or industry. These are the people you want to network with to learn more about a particular business or to grow in your current field.

Research Triangle Park...

The business and industry located in the area of Raleigh, Durham, and Chapel Hill, North Carolina. This area is one of the leading high tech research and development centers in the country and home to a significant number of leading edge companies such as IBM, Cisco Systems, and GlaxoSmithKline.

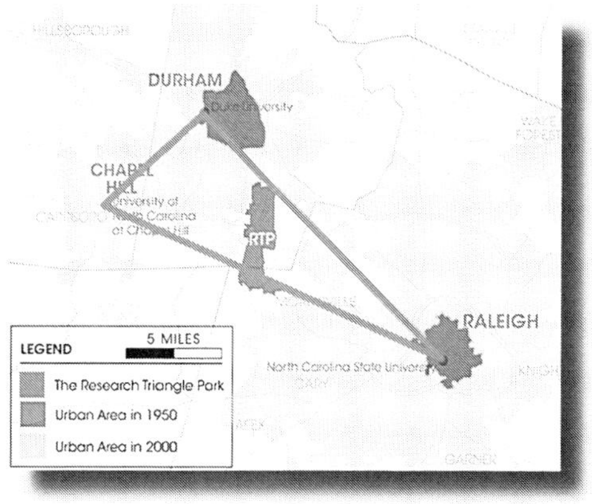

Silicon Valley...

Located in San Francisco, California, this is the main hub for major U.S. technology companies. So what's with the name? California's known for its valley-filled landscape and computers are known for their silicone components!

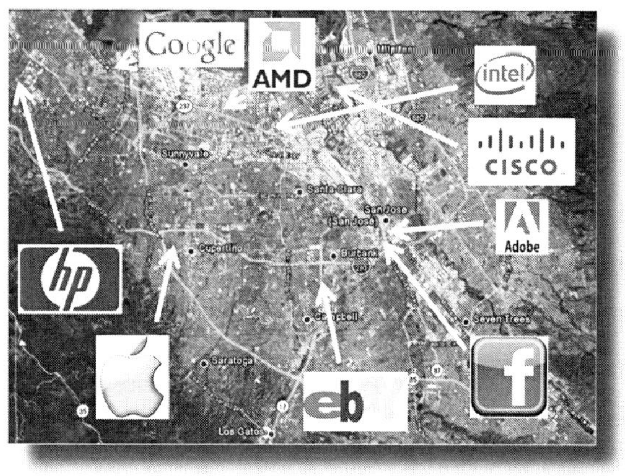

Steve...

Steve Jobs of Apple fame who gave us the first real personal computer—the "Mac".

Wall Street...

Not a street of walls, but the street in New York that is the main location for the United States Stock Market. It can also refer to the banks, bigger businesses and corporations, and other large and powerful groups related to the economy.

Warren...

That's Warren Buffet, the "Oracle of Omaha" who is a stock genius, owns loads of companies, and is full of wit and wisdom, as in "Warren says..."

Jack Welch...

Former CEO of General Electric who raised the company's value by an extraordinary percentage during his time there.

World Wide Web...

The internet in all its glory!

Mark Zuckerberg...

Cofounder and current CEO of our beloved Facebook. Without him and the other cofounders, we might all still be relying on Myspace to keep track of each other (And how unfortunate would that be?).

JOB INTERVIEW: a probably nerve-wracking experience in which a hopeful job candidate sits in front of a Human Resources Director and tries to answer questions correctly while trying not to visibly sweat, shake, have voice crack, or cry. Really, it's not that bad!

Carole Marsh's CAREERS CURRICULUM™

FOR MIDDLE SCHOOL, HIGH SCHOOL, COLLEGE AND **BEYOND!**

"If you are ready for 'readiness'...for choosing a career pathway... deciding what to do after high school...or for a first job, or raise and promotion - THIS SERIES IS FOR YOU!"

– James Barnard

Job Tracks: 60* Great Careers and How to Get from Where You Are... to Where You Want To Go!

This book is filled with unique and effective approaches for helping students find their career pathway! Featuring 60 careers from today's job market, this book allows young people to hear first-hand from a person with the job: how they got it, what they do, what education and skills were required, and "what I would have done differently!" Readers get the feel of what particular careers might actually be like—essential knowledge for that all-important decision!

"Entertaining and charming to read!"

Essential Skills for the Real World of Work: Things EVERY Student Must Know!

There's no other book that does a better job of sharing essential skills for the real business world and explaining why they are essential! This book dishes out the subtleties, nuances, and in between-the-lines considerations of job interviewers who are not only interested in candidates with essential skills, but are actually desperate for them! It includes a fun and effective scoring system to encourage students to rack up job-readiness skills long before they are required.

"Highly encouraging and enlightening!"

Would You Hire This Person? A Look at Getting Hired (or Not!)...from the Point of View of Your (Possible!) Future Employer

Read verbatim interviews that are both entertaining and enlightening! In this book, students hear both sides of the interview, including the employer and job candidate's unspoken thoughts. The reader can decide for himself or herself if they would hire the job candidate before learning the actual outcome.

"Such realistic scenarios – I got nervous reading them! I wanted the person to get the job, but, gee...I can see why some would not!"

www.careerscurriculum.com

Work Words: Job/Business/Career Words & Terms You Need to Know!

Get ready for lots of insider information and a few inside jokes! Written by a real employer, this book defines essential job, business, and career words and terms with insight, humor, and pizzazz! The contents of the book are organized into entertaining and effective groupings.

"Why be embarrassed when you can be empowered by knowing 'job speak' BEFORE you even get the job?"

Business Ethics & Etiquette for Students: You MUST Know These!

This highly entertaining and immensely practical book is an eye-opening must-read for students and new hires! It provides them with the confidence to avoid embarrassment, misstep, lost opportunity, and more.

"Fascinating and quite a lot of material covered. Anyone can benefit from this double-whammy of info book!"

The Parent and Teacher's Guide: Helping Students Navigate the Bumpy Road from School to More School, First Job, and Career

Filled with candid help from someone who has traveled the bumpy road of "non-readiness" from school to job to career, this book boasts timely and honest information that will help kids get ready for the real world of work. The wealth of ideas available to parents and teachers in this book will help them to navigate their student's journey ahead!

"Marsh has a keen sense of devotion to every type of student truly seeking a path to success. This book is worth the price for the compassion and humor, explanation of 'Rigor vs. Rigor Mortis,' and 'Why Study These Subjects' section. She's clearly 'been there, done that,' and achieved great success despite many obstacles!"

Carole Marsh's CAREERS CURRICULUM™

PLEASE CONTINUE TO VISIT OUR WEBSITE FOR MORE K-12 PRODUCTS IN PRINT & ONLINE FORMATS, INCLUDING:

- INDIVIDUAL CAREER MANUAL
- SCHOOL INFORMATION SHEETS
- COMPANY PROFILE SHEETS
- MAP OF OPPORTUNITIES
- ESSENTIAL SKILLS PASSPORT BOOK

... AND MUCH MORE!!

FOR MIDDLE SCHOOL, HIGH SCHOOL, COLLEGE AND **BEYOND!**

www.careerscurriculum.com